**University
of Michigan
Business
School** Management Series

INNOVATIVE SOLUTIONS TO THE
PRESSING PROBLEMS OF BUSINESS

The mission of the University of Michigan Business School Management Series is to provide accessible, practical, and cutting-edge solutions to the most critical challenges facing businesspeople today. The UMBS Management Series provides concepts and tools for people who seek to make a significant difference in their organizations. Drawing on the research and experience of faculty at The University of Michigan Business School, the books are written to stretch thinking while providing practical, focused, and innovative solutions to the pressing problems of business.

Also available in the UMBS series:

For additional information on any of these titles or future
titles in the series, visit www.umbsbooks.com.

Executive Summary

This is a book on how to use the interview process to select good people and to manage their performance. Using the Strategic Interviewing Approach will not only improve your ability to attract and retain good people, it will also help you coach, counsel, delegate, and provide feedback more effectively. You will be leveraging the knowledge from the interview process to support these management activities and you will be sending an important message to candidates about how you manage and what is important to your organization.

The book describes the six steps in the Strategic Interviewing Approach:

1. Develop realistic goals and manage the interview process. (Chapter Two)
2. Clearly define the performance expectations needed to perform the job successfully. (Chapter Three)
3. Ask questions that predict the candidate's ability to meet performance standards. (Chapter Four)
4. Decide on the answers you want before you ask the questions. (Chapter Four)

5. Conduct the interview in a manner that maximizes effective communication and accurate measurement. (Chapter Five)
6. Use behavioral decision making to predict the candidate's performance on the job. (Chapter Six)

For each step we provide strategies to help you complete the process. The strategies you adopt will depend on the specifics of your situation, particularly the performance expectations of the job you are trying to fill. But overall, your interview process will no longer be driven by the candidate's résumé, but rather by your company's performance expectations. Your new strategies will also improve your ability to attract, retain, and manage your employees.

The Strategic Interviewing Approach applies to technical and nontechnical jobs and across all organizational levels. At the end of each chapter, you will learn how three organizations, Old Kent Financial Services, Plante & Moran, and the International Monetary Fund, have implemented Strategic Interviewing within their respective organizations.

If you are an experienced interviewer, the approach will build on your experiences to enhance how you conduct interviews and manage the overall process. If you have not conducted many interviews or if you interview only occasionally, the approach will get you on the right track.

Finally, in the last chapter we will identify the signs of success that will let you know that you are making the best use of the Strategic Interviewing Approach.

Strategic Interviewing

How to Hire Good People

Richaurd Camp
Mary E. Vielhaber
Jack L. Simonetti

 JOSSEY-BASS
A Wiley Company
San Francisco

Published by Jossey-Bass
A Wiley Imprint
989 Market Street, San Francisco, CA 94103-1741   www.josseybass.com

Jossey-Bass books and products are available through most bookstores. To contact Jossey-Bass directly
call our Customer Care Department within the U.S. at (800) 956-7739, outside the U.S. at (317) 572-
3986 or fax (317) 572-4002.

Jossey-Bass also publishes its books in a variety of electronic formats. Some content that appears in
print may not be available in electronic books.

Library of Congress Cataloging-in-Publication Data

Camp, Richaurd R.
   Strategic interviewing: how to hire good people / Richaurd
Camp, Mary E. Vielhaber, Jack L. Simonetti.
   p. cm.
Includes bibliographical references and index.
   ISBN 0-7879-5394-6 (perm. paper)
1. Employment interviewing. I. Vielhaber, Mary E., date. II. Simonetti, Jack L. III. Title.
   HF5549.5.I6 C354 2001
   658.3'1124—dc21   2001000033

Printed in the United States of America
FIRST EDITION
HB Printing   10 9 8 7 6 5 4 3

Contents

To Kate, Bailey ("the boon"), Lauren, and Peggy.
I lack the words to tell you how much your love,
support, and patience means to me. I would like each
of you to know that it does not go unnoticed.
—Rick Camp

To Betty and Al Vielhaber,
for your continuous love and support.
—Mary Vielhaber

To my family, friends, and mentors for all
their support in making this book a reality.
—Jack Simonetti

Series Foreword

Welcome to the University of Michigan Business School Management Series. The books in this series address the most urgent problems facing business today. The series is part of a larger initiative at the University of Michigan Business School (UMBS) that ties together a range of efforts to create and share knowledge through conferences, survey research, interactive and distance training, print publications, and new media.

It is just this type of broad-based initiative that sparked my love affair with UMBS in 1984. From the day I arrived I was enamored with the quality of the research, the quality of the MBA program, and the quality of the Executive Education Center. Here was a business school committed to new lines of research, new ways of teaching, and the practical application of ideas. It was a place where innovative thinking could result in tangible outcomes.

The UMBS Management Series is one very important outcome, and it has an interesting history. It turns out that every year five thousand participants in our executive program fill out a marketing survey in which they write statements indicating the most important problems they face. One day Lucy Chin, one of our administrators, handed me a document containing all these statements. A content analysis of the data resulted in a list of forty-five pressing problems. The topics ranged from growing a company to managing personal stress. The list covered a wide territory, and I started to see its potential. People in organizations tend to be driven by a very traditional set of problems, but the solutions evolve. I went to my friends at Jossey-Bass to discuss a publishing project. The discussion eventually grew into the University of Michigan Business School Management Series— Innovative Solutions to the Pressing Problems of Business.

The books are independent of each other, but collectively they create a comprehensive set of management tools that cut across all the functional areas of business—from strategy to human resources to finance, accounting, and operations. They draw on the interdisciplinary research of the Michigan faculty. Yet each book is written so a serious manager can read it quickly and act immediately. I think you will find that they are books that will make a significant difference to you and your organization.

Robert E. Quinn, Consulting Editor
M.E. Tracy Distinguished Professor
University of Michigan Business School

Preface

For nearly fifteen years, we have been teaching the Strategic Interviewing Approach in seminars for Executive Education at the University of Michigan. Recruiters, human resources professionals, and hiring managers have consistently told us they were looking for an approach to interviewing that led to more objective decision making—and, more important, to good employees who performed well and stayed on the job. Whether for top executive or critical entry-level positions, highly technical jobs or ones that use more "soft" skills, organizations today are desperately seeking ways to identify good people who can not only meet but exceed expectations.

We wrote this book because we have seen how the Strategic Interviewing Approach can lead to better selection and help you attract and retain high-quality employees. We have also seen how this process leverages the knowledge from interviews to help managers coach, counsel, delegate, and conduct performance appraisals more effectively. Given the increasing demands on their time, managers need to integrate the various activities they do to manage performance. This approach helps managers make the best use of performance information.

As we have worked with interviewers, we have discovered that some of them are convinced that simply using behaviorally based questions is the key to success. While we also adopt a behaviorally based approach, we demonstrate that the strategic links between performance expectations, questions, and answers are key components of effective interviewing. Focusing on behavior is not enough if the behaviors you focus on are not the predictors of success on the job.

Throughout the book, we emphasize the need to define the components of performance expectations that demonstrate what a candidate needs to do to be successful on the job. We show you how to use clear performance expectations to drive the questions you ask, the answers that you are looking for, and the hiring decisions you make. Our goal is to give you a step-by-step approach and to coach you through the Strategic Interviewing Approach:

1. Develop realistic goals and manage the interview process.
2. Clearly define the performance expectations needed to perform the job successfully.
3. Develop and ask questions that are connected to your performance expectations and predict the candidate's ability to meet performance standards.
4. Decide on the answers you want before you ask the questions.
5. Conduct the interview in a manner that maximizes effective communication and accurate measurement.
6. Use behavioral decision making to predict the candidate's performance on the job.

Each chapter contains self-assessments and questions to help you evaluate your current approach and identify areas for development. The "Perspectives" sections at the end of each chapter provide examples of how three different organizations—Old Kent

Financial Services, Plante & Moran, and the International Monetary Fund—have implemented this approach to interviewing.*

With unemployment at its lowest levels in thirty years, employers today face a major challenge finding and retaining good employees. As you read this book, you will see how the use of the Strategic Interviewing Approach can significantly enhance the way you attract, select, and retain good people to your organization and manage them more effectively.

■ Acknowledgments

Many people have kindly shared their knowledge and contributed to this book. First, we thank Bob Quinn, the consulting editor for the University of Michigan Management Series, for developing the series and for encouraging us as we wrote this book. We also thank Susan Mason from Old Kent Financial Services, Susan Adams from the International Monetary Fund, and Mike Johnson from Plante & Moran for their insights and experiences in applying the Strategic Interviewing Approach. We applaud their skill and commitment to improving the interview process within their respective organizations.

Four very special colleagues and friends, Denise Tanguay, Nick Blanchard, and Fraya Wagner-Marsh from Eastern Michigan University and Claudio Fernández-Araóz from Egon-Zehnder International, provided their support and comments as we developed our perspectives on interviewing. We thank them for their insights and friendship. We also thank all of the participants from our Strategic Interviewing Seminars at the University of

*Note: The International Monetary Fund does not endorse any particular interviewing technique, nor does it endorse the authors' courses or those of the University of Michigan Executive Program.

Michigan and from individual training we have done within organizations. Their questions and comments helped us refine our approach to teaching interviewing. We especially thank the development editors from Jossey-Bass, Alan Venable and John Bergez. Their contributions are beyond words.

February 2001   Richaurd Camp
West Bloomfield, Michigan

Mary E. Vielhaber
Ann Arbor, Michigan

Jack L. Simonetti
Toledo, Ohio

Strategic Interviewing

The Case for a Strategic Interviewing Approach

You know the value of good employees. They make a difference through their job performance. They stand out from others in comparable jobs and produce the desired results. If you are like most employers, your selection process for new employees relies on the employment interview. This book explains how to make the best use of interviewing not only to select and retain employees who possess the right combination of skills, knowledge, attitudes, and values to contribute to your organization's success but also to reap additional organizational and departmental benefits.

The book describes what we call the Strategic Interviewing Approach. Across all organizational levels, this approach applies to jobs with performance standards that allow differentiation between effective and ineffective employees. The approach is not aimed at selecting employees for low-skill jobs, about whom an interview process may add little information by which to differentiate among applicants. Rather, it is aimed at hiring employees for positions in which performance makes a substantial difference and in which a good employee stands out. The interviewing techniques in this book will help you identify candidates who can meet and exceed performance standards. The techniques will also improve your ability to manage performance once people are hired.

Almost certainly in your company, it is your hiring managers who must make the final selection decision about new employees to hire for their departments. These managers need a strategy for removing subjectivity from their decisions so that they can objectively select more qualified candidates. The Strategic Interviewing Approach will help managers hire candidates with better qualifications and manage their performance better. In turn, the newly hired employees will be more likely to stay in the organization. In addition, human resource professionals and recruiters who use interviewing to identify candidates for hiring managers will find that the Strategic Interviewing Approach saves them time, money, and effort by providing a system for targeting qualified candidates.

This first chapter will explain why talented employees are so rare and why typical interviewing often fails to identify candidates who match the job requirements. The chapter will also introduce the Strategic Interviewing Approach.

■ The Current Crisis in Hiring

With a rapidly expanding economy and unemployment at its lowest levels in thirty years, employers today face a major challenge finding and retaining employees who will be effective within their organizations. In a speech to bankers in 1999, Federal Reserve Chairman Alan Greenspan acknowledged that the U.S. economy is "steadily depleting the pool of available workers."[1] Employers of all kinds are finding it harder and harder to keep an adequate number of employees, let alone talented ones. Fast food restaurants and retail stores are continually looking for entry-level employees. Companies that hire highly trained researchers and technicians face fierce competition for talented people. Executive and management recruiters do a booming business shifting the limited pool of qualified talent from one organization to another. Internal recruiters complain that they are overwhelmed with positions to fill for managers who appear to believe that there are numerous candidates from whom to select. Organizations discover that unless they can hire and retain effective employees, they are at a competitive disadvantage.

The U.S. Department of Labor estimates that it costs one-third of a new hire's annual salary to replace an employee. The tangible costs of turnover are the costs of recruiting, selection, and training. The intangible costs are lower productivity, increased workloads on remaining employees, lower morale, and adverse publicity. With national unemployment rates just over 4 percent, organizations with high turnover because of poor hiring decisions find they cannot compete effectively for skilled employees. For many industries including fast food, retail, convenience stores, trucking, and health care, annual turnover rates are more than 75 percent.

Why Good Candidates Are Rarer Than Ever

The changing blend of skills needed in the workplace contributes to the challenge of finding and keeping good employees. Increasing technology requirements for most jobs are barriers for new high school graduates who have not developed strong technical skills. They are also barriers for employees who have spent many years in low-tech jobs—their skills have simply not kept up with the needs of the workplace. A continued lack of qualified technical and professional workers is predicted for the twenty-first century.

In the past, many organizations and employees had a "womb-to-tomb" mentality. Employees hired in their youth expected the organization to demonstrate its loyalty by guaranteeing them a comfortable retirement after a long and successful career. Today, this mentality is rare. Organizations show less and less loyalty to employees, downsizing and restructuring to cut labor costs. Employees show less and less loyalty to their employers, moving more often from job to job. Even when you manage to hire good employees, you have no guarantee that they will stay.

New and Greater Demands on Selection Interviewing

Despite barriers to staffing an organization effectively, qualified candidates are available. The challenge for employers is to identify, hire, and retain them. These complicated tasks require the hiring organization to perform a wide range of actions, such as finding sources of good candidates, offering the right types of incentives, and providing an attractive work environment. Flexibility is key. No one set of methods is right for all situations, and what seems to be the best way today may not be the best way tomorrow. In addition, an effective source for one type of job may not be a good source for another. For example, Web-based job ads may be necessary to help an employer locate technically trained applicants, while traditional advertisements in newspapers typically generate candidates for low-skill jobs.

One common characteristic of highly skilled applicants is their desire to find a job that encourages them to demonstrate their capabilities and be successful. An organization can entice highly qualified candidates by the ways in which it defines success and measures it. Think about yourself. Would you want to join an organization (regardless of the rewards or work environment) if you couldn't use your skills and had no chance to succeed?

In essence, effective recruiting and retention send a message to applicants that your organization knows what kind of employees it wants and how to recruit, hire, and retain them. Additionally, organizations that clearly define what they want from applicants and know how to measure it accurately should have a better pool of interested applicants.

■ Why Interviewing Often Fails

It's useful to look at some of the reasons why selection interviewing often fails to meet the needs of an organization and the people being interviewed.

Illusions of Easiness

Interviewing is a hard task that many people think is easy. Why do people sometimes think that they are better interviewers than they really are? Perhaps one of the biggest reasons is that people don't really understand the purpose of an interview. Over the years in consulting with organizations, we have talked to many people who conduct interviews for a living. When we asked these human resource professionals how they got into their profession, they often say something like, "My boss told me that I was good at talking to people, and an interview is just a conversation." In truth, an interview is much more than a conversation, and good conversationalists aren't necessarily good interviewers.

Some managers admit that they like to play the role of psychologist. Without any of the required training and experience, they believe they can read behind interviewees' responses and know what they are really saying. By examining body language, particularly eye contact and tone of voice, managers believe they can tell who is telling the truth and who is telling a lie. Research evidence suggests, however, that this kind of judgment is more difficult than many managers think. For example, even when told that candidates may be lying, managers do not improve their ability to detect deception.[2]

Likewise, by playing psychologist, managers believe they can assess whether the applicant's personality will fit the organization's culture. Although research indicates that managers can identify differences in personality between applicants,[3] they appear to be unable to match the optimal personality type that will produce desired organizational outcomes.[4] In other words, managers may notice personality differences in candidates, but they typically don't know how to match the right personality for a particular job.

Another reason people think interviewing is easy is that they do not distinguish between forming personal judgments and actually assessing a candidate's competencies. Think about your own experiences. When you meet new people, do you form an opinion of them relatively quickly? If so, you are like most interviewers. The fallacy in this thinking is that forming an initial impression, as people do every day in a variety of circumstances, is not the same as predicting performance on the job.

People form impressions of each other, typically from what they observe about other people's speech, dress, or mannerisms. Their impressions are not necessarily right or wrong—they are simply impressions. The purpose of an interview, however, is to gather objective information that goes beyond first impressions. An interview is a test of the interviewer's ability to predict the candidate's performance on the job. The interviewer passes the test by hiring someone who does an excellent job, and fails the test by hiring a poor performer.

To understand the difference between forming impressions and interviewing, think of a good friend of yours whom you have seen in various situations and talked to on a variety of subjects, and who has even shared secrets with you. Has that friend ever done something that you never would have predicted? If so, perhaps you can see why interviewing is so difficult. If you can't always predict a close friend's behavior, how can you talk to someone new for perhaps half an hour and be able to predict their performance in a complex, perhaps stressful job?

Many hiring managers think that they are good interviewers because they equate interviewing with the ability to judge character. People in general tend to believe that they have naturally selected good friends, significant others, or spouses. Yet the standard they use for these selections—do I like this person?—does not apply to selecting employees. Interviewers should be selecting employees based on ability to do the job in question, not on personal preferences.

Most people who play golf on weekends recognize that they are not Tiger Woods. Most people who grill hot dogs occasionally recognize that they are not Julia Child. The duffer versus the pro golfer, the barbecue cook versus the gourmet chef: each member of each pair goes through the same steps, but has vastly different standards and desires vastly different outcomes. Likewise, an interviewer selecting an employee should have completely different standards and a completely different outcome in mind than when selecting a friend.

Shortcomings of Typical Selection Interviews

A typical interviewing process involves several people interviewing a candidate in separate, back-to-back interviews. Test your knowledge about employment interviewing by marking the statements in Assessment 1.1 as facts or fallacies.

⊡

■ Assessment 1.1. Interviewing Facts and Fallacies ■

1. The typical employment interview process
   provides a consistent (reliable) assessment
   of a candidate's ability to do the job.   □ Fact   □ Fallacy

2. During the typical interview, the interviewer
   tends to do the majority of the talking.   □ Fact   □ Fallacy

3. During the typical interview, the interviewer
   tends to weigh negative information more heavily
   than positive information.   □ Fact   □ Fallacy

4. During the typical interview, the interviewer's
   decision is made relatively early in the interview.   □ Fact   □ Fallacy

5. The typical employment interview process
   provides an accurate (valid) prediction of a
   candidate's ability to do the job.   □ Fact   □ Fallacy

Statement 1 is a fallacy. Interviewers who conduct one-on-one, back-to-back interviews will typically disagree in their assessments of the candidate. They often use different questions to gather information and different standards to assess the candidate, and so make different judgments. Reliable assessments are impossible with such inconsistency. Yet in a recent survey, most interviewers disagreed with the proposition that interviewers should ask the same questions across all applicants and should stick to specific job qualifications.[5]

Statements 2, 3, and 4 are facts. The typical interviewer does most of the talking.[6] Because interviewers often confuse an interview with a conversation, the interviewer will spend most of the time talking about the job rather than assessing the candidate's fit for the job. The typical interviewer also tends to weigh negative information more heavily than positive information. Many interviewers search for a reason to reject the candidate.[7] They often make the hiring decision early in the interview process and look for evidence to support their decision.[8]

Statements 2, 3, and 4 represent three common interviewing errors. Recognizing these and similar problems is a good place to start improving the process.

Statement 5 is a fallacy. But why would intelligent businesspeople use a technique that does not produce good results? The most likely reason is that interviews are easy to conduct. Because nearly anyone can ask questions and make a judgment, managers believe they are using an effective selection technique. Evidence exists that interviews have the potential to be effective.[9] However, Robert Guion, one of the most respected researchers in the field of employee selection, commenting on developments in interviewing approaches, noted: "These developments probably influence researchers without having much influence on the way most interviews were—or still are—conducted: haphazard, idiosyncratic, and spur of the moment. My hunch is that interviews in general are no better but that the literature available for reviewers to survey has improved. If so, we probably know a lot more about assessment by interviewing, and how to make valid interview-based decisions, than we have communicated to the world at large—where (I suspect) poor interviews remain the rule."[10]

The truth is that unless you have carefully determined your performance expectations and developed questions and standards to assess whether the candidate can meet the expectations, you will not be able to make an accurate selection decision. By following the Strategic Interviewing Approach presented in this book, however, you can improve the reliability and accuracy of interviews and make better selections as a result.

Assessing Your Current Practice

Take a moment to assess your own interviewing approach. Have you used any of the interview questions in Assessment 1.2?

■ Assessment 1.2. ■
Assess Your Own Approach to Interviewing

1. What is your strength (or weakness)?
   - ☐ Never use this question.
   - ☐ Sometimes use this question.
   - ☐ Always use this question.

2. Where do you want to be five years from now?
   - ☐ Never use this question.
   - ☐ Sometimes use this question.
   - ☐ Always use this question.

3. Why should I hire you?
   - ☐ Never use this question.
   - ☐ Sometimes use this question.
   - ☐ Always use this question.

4. What is your ideal job?
   - ☐ Never use this question.
   - ☐ Sometimes use this question.
   - ☐ Always use this question.

5. If you had to pick one, what kind of a (vegetable, fruit, tree, whatever) would you be and why?
   - ☐ Never use this question.
   - ☐ Sometimes use this question.
   - ☐ Always use this question.

All these questions are ineffective, but interviewers commonly use them to assess candidates for jobs at various levels in organizations.[11] Many interviewers who attend our interviewing seminars cite these as examples of the best questions they have ever asked or been asked in an interview. Part of the reason for using these types of questions and believing they are effective is sheer repetition and familiarity. Since an employer may have asked you these questions, you might repeat them when you move to the role of interviewer. This is a very common pattern—think of the old adage that says that you can't go swimming until an hour after you eat. Though there is no scientific support for the warning, people may still behave as if it is true because they've heard it so many times.

Hiding Out Versus Getting Better

Historically, poor interviewers have been able to hide their flaws. In the 1960s and 1970s, jobs were simpler and did not change as rapidly. Also, skills were more uniform in the workforce. People were more likely to be qualified for a job because, unlike today, highly job-specific job requirements were minimal. If you interviewed ten candidates for a job, most of them would be qualified. As a result, poor interviewers had a much higher chance of finding qualified candidates. They were more likely to make effective decisions, even by an ineffective process.

Today, fewer workers can be classed as highly skilled for any given job. If you interview ten candidates, few if any may meet all of the job's requirements. No longer is the poor interviewer likely to make a good decision so easily. Meanwhile, the cost of failing to find a good employee is greater, since so many companies have downsized to reduce personnel. If you hire an unqualified person, the burden of supporting that person is shared by fewer people. In addition, there is the lost opportunity cost of failing to find the talented employee who will give your organization a competitive edge.

■ A Strategic Approach to Interviewing

This book provides a strategic approach to interviewing based on a six-step process. The Strategic Interviewing Approach focuses on behaviors rather than subjective impressions. Also, it uses a variety of measurements to assess the match between a candidate's competencies and the level of performance expected on the job. Strategic interviews link key performance expectations to questions, answers, and assessments.

For managers and interviewers who lack training, the Strategic Interviewing Approach offers a systematic, research-based method for selecting employees. For those who have been trained in other interviewing methods, the approach will provide the foundation for new strategies for recruiting, selecting, and developing good employees. Exhibit 1.1 summarizes the approach.

The next five chapters describe the steps of this approach in detail. Chapter Two deals with Step 1 and describes strategies for developing realistic goals and managing the interviewing process. It also demonstrates how interviewers often pack more into the interview than the interview is capable of covering. The chapter will include questions to help you assess if this is a problem with your interviews.

Chapter Three addresses Step 2. It will help you describe the key aspects of the job that the person you hire will do. Some people say that they don't hire a person for a particular job, but for a career. But since a career is a series of jobs, this is a distinction without a difference. You hire someone to do something. If you don't know what the something is that the person is going to do, how can you determine whether they will be good at doing it?

Exhibit 1.1. The Strategic Interviewing Approach

1. Develop realistic goals and manage the interview process.

2. Clearly define the performance expectations needed to perform the job successfully.

3. Ask questions that predict the candidate's ability to meet performance standards.

4. Decide on the answers you want before you ask the questions.

5. Conduct the interview in a manner that maximizes effective communication and accurate measurement.

6. Use behavioral decision making to predict the candidate's performance on the job.

Chapter Three will also help you clearly define the performance expectations that a candidate must meet in order to succeed. Knowing what someone needs to do is not the same as knowing what it takes to do it. For example, many baseball fans know what a good baseball manager needs to do (Step 2). The manager may need to shift fielders so they are in the right position for the batter, take out pitchers who have lost their "stuff," or choose the right pinch hitter to match the pitcher. But what must a manager know in order to do these things? These are part of the job's performance expectations and they will vary depending on how you define success.

Chapter Four will focus on Step 3, and will help you develop questions that predict the candidate's ability to meet the performance expectations needed to perform the job effectively. The connection between the question and the aspects of job performance it predicts is a key theme of this book. In the Strategic Interviewing Approach, interviewers need to know why they are asking a question in an interview, what it measures, and what it will predict about the candidate's ability to do the job.

The chapter also addresses Step 4 of the process, and will help you develop the right answers before you ask the questions. Interviewers sometimes say that the questions that they ask do not have right or wrong answers, but are designed to get a "feel for the candidate." Again, this is a distinction without a difference, since a "right feel" probably indicates that the person gave a right answer and the "wrong feel" probably indicates the opposite. Interviewers have absolutely no choice about whether to develop correct answers to the questions they ask. The only choice is when to develop these answers. The chapter will demonstrate why interviewers who elect not to come up with the correct answers until after they have asked their questions run a high risk of letting the candidates set the performance standards for the position.

Thus Chapters Two though Four cover Steps 1 through 4 of the Strategic Interviewing Approach, preparing for an effective interview. An interviewer who doesn't prepare with these steps is unlikely to have a successful interview. Of course, even when the interviewer prepares thoroughly, if the interview is not properly conducted, it is still likely to fail. Chapter Five will address Step 5 and will demonstrate how to conduct the interview in a way that maximizes effective communication and accurate measurement.

Additionally, Chapter Five tells how to conduct team interviews and describes their advantages and disadvantages. The chapter gives particular attention to the benefits versus the costs of team interviews. Managers will learn strategies for improving both the process and the results of team interviews.

Chapter Six presents Step 6 and shows how to make a behavioral decision based on the information gathered in the interview. It will describe judgment errors that many interviewers make that can negate the benefits of an otherwise effective process. The chapter will also present specific strategies for focusing the hiring decision on the match between the applicant's past behaviors and the job's performance expectations.

Finally, Chapter Seven will answer some of the typical questions people have raised about the challenges in implementing this interviewing process. It will also highlight the signs of success that let interviewers know if they are effectively implementing the Strategic Interviewing Approach.

■ Is This Approach Worth Learning?

You may be thinking at this point, "The six steps make sense, but I don't hire that many people in a year. Is all this worth my effort to learn?" You may not hire a large number of people in a year, but if you are a hiring manager or aspire to be one, learning the techniques in this book will definitely be worth your time and effort. Even managers who do not conduct selection interviews can benefit from the Strategic Interviewing Approach.

Every manager frequently delegates work. Delegation is really a mini-selection process, in which the manager determines the performance requirements for the assignment and matches the right person to that assignment based on the match between the performance requirements and the worker's competency. If you follow the process outlined in this book, you will not only improve your interviewing, you will improve how you delegate work assignments.

Using the techniques in this book can also improve the way managers train and coach employees. Effective training begins with a needs assessment that identifies what you expect employees to do once they are trained. Defining competencies for interviewing and defining training needs will provide information for clear performance standards. In turn, the performance standards can serve as guidelines for coaching employees for better on-the-job performance.

Another positive outcome of following this process is that you will be able to do a better job of measuring employee performance. If you hire an applicant, you are predicting that the person will succeed on the job. But one of the problems in assessing performance is that managers often do not clearly specify their performance standards. The Strategic Interviewing Approach helps the employer determine those standards. With clearly defined standards, you will also improve how you conduct performance appraisals, coach employees, and provide feedback. As a result, you will most likely have a wider pool of interested applicants from which to select.

What Are the Benefits of the Strategic Interviewing Approach Compared with Other Interviewing Approaches?

Like most contemporary approaches to interviewing, the Strategic Interviewing Approach is behaviorally based: it assumes that past behavior is the best predictor of future behavior. However, it offers several advantages over other approaches:

- It focuses on more than just developing questions and provides strategies to manage each step of the process.
- It recognizes that all the steps are interconnected.
- It is closely related to other aspects of performance management such as performance appraisal, training, coaching, and delegation. The Strategic Interviewing Approach leverages the learning from the interviewing process to enhance these activities.
- It makes strategic connections between the question, the aspect of the job performance that the question is designed to predict, and the right answer. Many interviewers ask behavioral questions without fully understanding the strategy behind the questions. The Strategic Interviewing Approach helps the interviewer know what answer will predict the applicant's job performance and what statement will indicate that the person can or cannot do the job.
- It provides a sound basis for making decisions based on behavior and predicts the applicant's future performance based on the candidate's past behavior.
- Multiple interviewers involved in a selection decision will have the same standards for the job and so improve the reliability of the selection decision.

The Strategic Interviewing Approach has many other benefits for hiring managers and human resource professionals. By using the strategies in this approach, you will reduce the subjectivity of your hiring decisions and improve the accuracy of your selection decisions. By making better selection decisions, you will be hiring employees who can contribute more quickly to your organization. More important, you will be able to reduce turnover costs that drain your profits.

Demonstrated Success of the Strategic Interviewing Approach

The strategies described in this book use the contemporary approaches to interviewing that have been shown by both research and practice to apply across organizational levels and positions, in different types of organizations, and even across national boundaries.[12] Managers, human resource professionals, and executive recruiters in countries throughout North and South America, Europe, and Asia have used the Strategic Interviewing Approach to select employees from entry level to corporate president, and for jobs ranging from information technologists to nurses, writers, and artists. You may need to consider minor variations based on the organizational level, type of company, or country, but the basic approach to Strategic Interviewing will work in any situation where you need to hire and retain good employees. In the "Perspectives" section at the end of each chapter, you will find the views of professionals who have applied the Strategic Interviewing Approach in their organizations. Their comments will illustrate how this interviewing approach has worked for them.

CHAPTER SUMMARY

Attracting, selecting, and retaining a talented workforce will continue to be one of management's most pressing problems in the years to come. Continuing low unemployment rates along with the war for talent created by an expanding economy have made it increasingly difficult to find effective employees. To address this problem, hiring managers and human resource professionals must have a strategy. While there are various strategies that an interviewer can use to conduct an effective interview, the Strategic Interviewing Approach will provide a systematic, research-based approach for selecting employees that meet the requirements of the job and the needs of the manager and the organization.

In the following section, senior executives from three different organizations share their perspectives on the benefits of the Strategic Interviewing Approach. A vice president of human resources from a large bank, a human resources manager from a large accounting firm and the chief of recruitment for the International Monetary Fund discuss why their organizations made the changes they did.

□

Perspectives on Strategic Interviewing

Susan Mason, Vice President of Human Resources,
Old Kent Financial Services

*Why did your organization change its approach to interviewing? What
was changed?*

At Old Kent, we altered our interviewing approach because of the
many benefits using the techniques of the Strategic Interviewing Approach. For us, what's most important is that we are selecting employees
based on their ability to perform well on the job rather than their ability
to interview well. This leads to better employment decisions, as well as
to reduced turnover and recruiting costs. We have been successful using
this approach in conjunction with other interviewing techniques.

With Strategic Interviewing, we use a structured interviewer guide
with targeted questions for each position. That gives a consistent interviewing experience for all of our applicants. We also know that the consistency allows us to treat each applicant fairly. We believe that consistency
supports Old Kent's objectives toward our employment decisions.

Targeted questions also reduce our time commitment for interviewing. In the past, we spent a lot of time conducting interviews but we didn't
always ask effective questions. Today, we ask job-related questions and
clearly we are able to make better employment choices. When candidates
are not selected, we can also provide coaching to help them understand
the skills they need to develop.

Hiring managers using this method are more analytical in their decision-making process. Rather than relying on their gut feelings, they have
more solid information they can use to make the decision. Instead of asking, "Do I like this candidate?" managers ask themselves, "Can this candidate do this job?"

Mike Johnson, Human Resources Manager, Plante & Moran

*Why did your organization change its approach to interviewing? What
was changed?*

In our accounting firm, our recruiting goal is to select the partners
of the future. For a number of reasons, that job is not as easy as it used
to be. One reason is that we are asking our partners to do more than ever

before and therefore it takes a bit longer to become partner. Since it takes longer to make partner, we have more invested in people and there are greater costs to the organization if someone doesn't make it.

The other factor is the severely limited talent pool to pick from. Fewer and fewer people are coming into the profession. This makes it much harder to find good people. We have to select people who can develop to meet our challenges. Previously, when there were greater numbers, this was much easier to do.

We feel we take a much more strategic approach to interviewing that ties in with our performance management system and the competencies associated with performance management. The same criteria that our interviewers use to evaluate people on campus are used to assess people in their day-to-day job performance. We think this has reinforced the understanding and use of the competencies as a driver for selection.

We are also not as likely to select what I would call the typical "Plante Moraners." We are not selecting people "just like us." The new system allows us to select people we wouldn't have selected in the past, but who are doing well with the firm. We are taking strategic chances on people. We're basing our decisions on hard facts that are much more critical to success. The ultimate measure of our success in this approach will be to what extent the people that we've been hiring make partner. One intermediate measure is that our turnover, in high turnover times, has been down for the first time in four years.

Susan J. Adams, Chief of Recruitment, International Monetary Fund

Why did your organization change its approach to interviewing? What was changed?

The IMF changed its approach to interviewing because we had too little consistency and quality control across interviewers in different departments. We began to change our approach by first getting the professional recruiters in the HR Department trained in the new technique, and then we taught it gradually to our line managers in both the headquarters and the field offices.

The biggest difference we have seen is that the comparison of candidates for a particular position is much more systematic and obvious than in the past, where personal judgments played far too great a role.

So far, the new process is meeting our expectations. It does take a fair amount of time to indoctrinate all of the possible interviewers in the organization into the new process. But we know it is working. In one recent case, we selected a candidate who answered the "critical situations" questions better than someone who had already acted in the job for several months (and should have answered those questions better!). In the past, we would have simply offered the job to the acting incumbent.

Applications

1. What's your current success rate in hiring and retaining the right people for your organization?
2. How well trained in interviewing are the people who do selection interviewing in your organization? Do you provide training in how to interview, for managers who make the hiring decisions?
3. How does your current interviewing process match up with the Strategic Interviewing Approach? What steps are you taking? What steps are you missing?

Developing Realistic Goals and Managing the Interview Process

What does it take to be a good interviewer? The answer depends on the goals you are trying to achieve through the interview process. People who think of an interview as simply a conversation rarely identify specific goals for their interviews. In this chapter, we will demonstrate that good interviewers develop realistic goals and manage the interview process. Good interviewers also need a range of skills and the ability to shift among a variety of perspectives to achieve their interviewing goals.

This chapter begins with the potential goals that interviewers have in mind when they interview an applicant for a job. An assessment is provided to help you evaluate the goals you set for your interviews and determine if they are realistic. We will also discuss the problems that occur when interviewers try to accomplish too much in a single interview or are not clear about what they need to achieve. Finally, we will present specific strategies for developing realistic goals and managing the interview process.

■ Potential Goals of Interviewing

Most interviewers focus on some combination of three interviewing goals. First, interviewers attempt to accurately measure whether the candidate has what it takes to do the job. Second, they try to influence the candidate's job decision by selling the positive features of the job and the organization. Third, they assist the candidate in making an appropriate job choice by providing a balanced view of the challenges and rewards of the job. At first glance, the three goals may seem to be contradictory. In this chapter, we will argue that if you manage the interview process, you will decrease the possibility that you are focusing on contradictory goals. As you read about each of these goals, think about what you are trying to achieve in your interviews.

Accurately Measuring Whether the Candidate Can Do the Job

Earlier we said that an interview is a test for the interviewer. It is also a test for the interviewee. Most people don't think of it that way, but it is really a test that measures whether someone has what the interviewer is looking for. You pass the test if you are hired; you fail if the interviewer determines you lack what is needed for the job.

Most interviewers would probably agree that they want the interview to be a test of whether the candidate can effectively perform the job. To measure whether the candidate can do the job requires that interviewers try to measure candidates on a variety of factors. For example, you probably would want to know if the candidate had the technical abilities to perform the job effectively, and if the person would fit into the culture and get along with the other workers and the boss.

As we noted in Chapter One, often the interview is an inaccurate measurement of the candidate's ability to perform the job. Instead of focusing on how the candidate is likely to behave on the job, many interviewers rely on impressions—what they like and what they don't like about the candidate.

Certainly not every job requires the interviewer to make an accurate measurement of the applicant's ability to do the job. In some jobs, particularly low-skill jobs, there is not much difference between good and minimally acceptable or even bad employees. The Strategic Interviewing Approach focuses on jobs where you can differentiate performance among employees. In the following chapters we will outline how to create this measurement to select good employees. For now, we suggest that accurate measurement is unlikely to occur unless interviewers realize that their interview goals should focus not on their likes and dislikes but on what is needed to be a good employee.

Influencing the Candidate's Job Choice

Convincing the applicant to accept the job if it is offered is another potential interviewing goal. To achieve this goal, interviewers sell the organization and the job to the candidate by painting a positive picture. Interviewers emphasize positive information such as the work the person will be doing, the comfortable working conditions, and the advantages of the company's location. They may also discuss future job opportunities within the company or the company's vision and future prospects. Because of its overwhelmingly positive nature, this information is often called *public relations* or simply *PR*. Human resource professionals and managers who attend our interviewing seminars at the University of Michigan say that they provide PR to persuade the candidate that their organization is a better place to work than other organizations that the candidate may be considering.

Accurately measuring whether the candidate can do the job is logically consistent with influencing a candidate to accept a job if it is offered. If the candidate can do the job, certainly the interviewer would want to recruit this person who is likely to be a good employee. However, interviewers need different strategies to attain these separate goals. Accurate measurement requires an objective, unbiased individual who will focus on the correct information—evidence of job-related skills. Influencing requires the interviewer to be an advocate and salesperson. Research indicates that interviewers act differently based on their objective. Interviewers who were focused on influence talked 50 percent more, volunteered twice as much information, and asked half as many questions as interviewers who were more focused on measurement.[1] Although many interviewers can focus on both goals, interviewers must recognize the strategy differences and make sure that their actions are consistent with their goals.

Assisting the Candidate in Making an Appropriate Job Choice

Most interviewers also try to provide realistic job information to candidates to help them make the decision about joining the organization. Typically, this information describes the specific job and situation that the applicant will face if hired. Many interviewers characterize this information as their attempt to give the applicant a *balanced view* of the job. The interviewers give a preview of the positives associated with the position along with the negatives (euphemized as the "challenges"). Negatives might include difficult working conditions, extensive travel on the job, or a history of conflict between departments. This type of balanced positive and negative job information is called a *realistic job preview* or *RJP*.[2]

Why would an interviewer provide the RJP instead of selling the candidate solely on the advantages of the position? If the goal is to get the candidate interested and "on board," why jeopardize success? Why provide applicants with impartial information that may lead to their rejecting the position? The reason to be honest about the negatives on the job is that you are interested not only in recruiting candidates but in retaining the ones you hire. More important, if people assume positions with a clear picture of what they will face, they will be more likely to manage the challenges.

The logic of realistic job previews is that if someone is going to quit, it is always best if they "quit" before they are hired. If an applicant withdraws from consideration after you have provided an RJP, you have helped them determine that the job is not a good match for them.

Alan G. Frost, director of management development for Home Depot, partially credits videos that give applicants a clear picture of the demands on the job with the retailer's 11.4 percent decline in employee turnover. According to Frost, store managers who are eager to hire may understate the stress of a job in order to fill the position. Although the candidate may temporarily solve the manager's need for employees, rapid turnover actually has many more costs besides the vacancy in the position.[3] Overall, the research on RJPs has shown mixed results in terms of impact on turnover. RJPs tend to work best for more intelligent, more committed, and more experienced applicants.[4]

Providing realistic job previews to assist the candidate in making an appropriate job choice requires strategies that are different from those for the two previous goals. In a sense, the interviewer becomes an advocate for the candidate, providing accurate information for making a good decision. Again, while it is possible to focus on this goal as well as the others in the same interview, interviewers must make sure that they use appropriate strategies for each goal. Interviewers need to be careful, however, not to become so much of an advocate for the candidate that they diminish the goal of accurate measurement.

■ Assessing the Time Spent on Achieving Your Interview Goals

Most interviewers do not take the time to think about their goals for an interview. They simply do it. Take a minute and use Assessment 2.1 to roughly estimate how much time you devote to the PR and RJP parts of your interviews. Column 1 lists some activities that occur in the interview, along with a brief description. In Column 2, record an estimate of how much time you would devote to each activity in a sixty-minute interview. If you manage other interviewers, use the assessment to audit how your in-

■ Assessment 2.1. ■ How Do You Spend Your Time in an Interview?	
Activity or Goal	Time You Typically Devote to this Activity
The beginning of the interview—making small talk and introducing the process for the interview.	
The end of the interview—closing it effectively.	
Providing an opportunity for the interviewee to ask questions.	
Influencing the candidate's job choice (PR).	
Assisting the candidate in making an appropriate job choice (RJP).	
Total interview time devoted to activities other than accurately measuring whether the candidate can do the job.	

terviewers typically use their time in interviews. Keep in mind that times may vary depending on the candidate and level of the job, but try to give typical numbers.

If you are like most interviewers, you estimated five to ten minutes for each activity. This means you probably spend between twenty-five and fifty minutes on activities other than measuring whether the candidate can do the job. As a result, in a typical sixty-minute interview, you have ten to thirty-five minutes left for measurement.

Now make another estimate in Assessment 2.2. How many different factors do you typically want to measure in the interview? Think about all of the different things that someone needs to know and be able to do if they are to do the job well. For example, technical knowledge and skill, attitudes, values, conflict resolution skills, leadership, decision-making skills, and team skills may be the factors you are measuring in candidates. Again, your answers will vary depending on the job, but make a quick estimate.

■ Assessment 2.2. ■

How Much Interviewing Time Do You Spend

Measuring Whether the Candidate Can Do the Job?

How many factors do you attempt to measure in a typical interview?	
How much time is left in a sixty-minute interview to assess each of these factors? (Subtract the number in the last line of Assessment 2.1 from 60.)	
On average, how much time can you spend per factor? (Divide the available interviewing time computed in the preceding row by the number of factors.)	

Your answer concerning the number of areas of measurement will most likely be anywhere from five to ten. Assuming you are measuring at least five factors, you have approximately two to seven minutes to measure each one. With more areas of measurement, you have even less time to measure each one.

Many interviewers are shocked when they complete these assessments and realize how little time they actually devote to measurement during the interview process. Often when we add up the time that interviewers estimate they devote to introductions, conclusions, PR, and RJP, we find that there is literally no time left for measurement! Clearly, you will have difficulty hiring good employees if you don't take the time to measure their ability to do the job. Although this is the most glaring problem, other problems typically occur when interviewers do not manage the interviewing process effectively.

■ Problems of Interview Management

Besides failing to measure candidates' capacity for the job at hand, poorly managed interviews lead to inconsistent or contradictory messages to candidates, and subject candidates to redundant interviews that focus on gathering the same information over and over again.[5] These problems are discussed in upcoming paragraphs.

Insufficient Time Devoted to Measurement

Not spending the time to adequately measure the candidate is a serious problem for interviewers who want to hire good employees. This problem may be linked to the fact that in the typical interview, the interviewer often does most of the talking. Why does this occur? We think that one major reason is that interviewers like to talk about things with which they feel comfortable. Measuring the candidate's ability to perform the job requires the interviewer to know what to ask and what to look for in the answers. Since the typical interviewer has not prepared for the interview and isn't trained on how to measure performance, the interviewer talks about the things he or she knows—the organization (PR) or the job (RJP).

If the interviewer has done most of the talking during the interview and there has been little time devoted to measurement, the interviewer has to rely on general impressions for the decision. We can't expect interviewers to accurately assess candidates if they haven't devoted the necessary time to gather the data needed for the decision.

Failure to manage the interview process is the source of this problem. Interviewers are often given wide discretion in how they conduct their interviews. Without guidance, they are often unfocused within their individual interviews. Likewise, there often is very little coordination among interviewers in the process. As a result, a lot of time is spent on interviewing candidates, but the time is not focused on accurate measurement.

Inconsistent, Contradictory, or Misleading Messages

Failure to manage the interview process among multiple interviewers can also contribute to a negative image of your organization by sending an inconsistent or contradictory message. Most organizations haven't really thought through their PR objectives for interviewing and therefore don't manage the PR message. As a result, different interviewers may send different messages to a single applicant. One interviewer can lead a candidate to believe there are opportunities for advancement while another interviewer may leave the candidate with the impression that few higher-level positions are filled from within.

Organizations often assume that their interviewers are capable and skilled in providing the appropriate public relations information to candidates. As a result, interviewer training rarely, if ever, includes strategies for creating an accurate image of the organization.

Organizations do not expect everyone who must communicate with the media to be skilled in relating the corporate image without training or experience. For that, they hire trained PR experts. But they do not apply the same logic to interviews. They seem to accept the likelihood that different interviewers will convey different—and sometimes contradictory—messages about the organization.

Some interviewers send messages to candidates that they think the candidate wants to hear, without solid evidence that these messages interest the candidate. For example, in an effort to persuade the interviewee to accept a job offer, interviewers will attempt to sell the organization with exaggerated claims about the organization's culture or opportunities for advancement. A candidate who accepts a job offer after such a sales job is apt to find out very quickly that the image created by the interviewer does not match the organization's reality. When the new employee leaves shortly after starting the job, the organization has not only lost an employee, it has also created a negative image that may hurt future recruiting efforts.

Too much selling also leads recruits to second thoughts about the organization. Researchers have found that the more time the interviewer spent selling the job, the less attractive applicants perceived the job to be. Applicants became suspicious as to why the job had to be sold so extensively.[6]

Redundant Interviews

As noted earlier, interviewees often go through a series of back-to-back interviews, hearing similar comments and answering similar generic questions in each interview. This is a waste of everyone's time. Applicants may need to hear some PR, but they don't need to hear the same message from multiple sources. Applicants may need to receive the RJP, but they don't need to hear it several times, especially when that time could be used for other important purposes.

Redundant interviews send a negative message about your organization. Interviewees are also assessing the organization as they are being assessed.[7] Think for a moment about the impressions that you want to give top quality candidates during the interview process. Then look at Table 2.1, which outlines a candidate's day for a typical on-site interview.

What impression do you think the candidate forms after a full day of back-to back interviews if most of the interviews

Table 2.1. Typical Interviewee Day for On-Site Visit

Time	Activity	Content
9 A.M.	Interview with Human Resources representative	Small amount of time devoted to outline of the day, most of the interview devoted to PR and the RJP. Little interview time devoted to competency assessment. This opening session may also include a brief tour of the facility and the department.
10 A.M.	Interview with hiring manager	Most of the interview devoted to PR and the RJP. Little interview time devoted to competency assessment.
11 A.M.	Interview with manager in related department	Most of the interview duplicates the earlier interviews.
Noon	Interview with peer	Most of the interview duplicates the earlier interviews.
1 P.M.	Lunch with hiring manager	Informal interview with more time devoted to candidate's own questions
2 P.M.	Interview with peer	Most of the interview duplicates the earlier interviews.
3 P.M.	Interview with peer	Most of the interview duplicates the earlier interviews.
4 P.M.	Interview with Human Resources representative	Closing interview, devoted to answering candidate's questions.

cover the same general topics? What impression would you form if you experienced this process? Do you get the message, "We are a high-quality organization where you will be accurately measured and rewarded?" If you want to be able to attract and retain top applicants, you have to be able to generate this impression. Hiring bonuses and other incentives to work in an organization lose much of their effectiveness if candidates do not feel the organization can accurately measure their performance. Applicants who undergo a day of back-to-back interviews with interviewers asking the same generic questions are likely to form the impression that this is an organization where qualifications are unimportant. If qualifications were important, the organization would devote more time to measuring applicants in a more systematic, objective interviewing process.[8] The more the interview process focuses on measurement versus recruiting, the more likely highly qualified applicants are to pursue a job.

■ Strategies for Managing the Interview Process

To address the problems of insufficient time devoted to measurement, inconsistent or contradictory messages, and redundant interviews, various strategies can be used at the individual and organizational levels to manage the interview process. At the same time, it is possible to maintain the interviewers' discretion in selecting candidates that meet their unique needs. For each strategy, we attempt to describe how it helps manage the interview process while allowing managers flexibility to address their particular concerns. As you read about each of the strategies, consider how you can use the strategies in your own interviewing process.

Strategy 1: Set Clear Goals for Each Interview

While we have noted that the goals of accurate measurement, influencing the candidate's job choice, and assisting the candidate in making an appropriate job choice are common to most interviews, the importance of these activities will vary based on the type of job and the situation of the organization. For example, for a job such as a high school or college internship, there may be little difference among the skill levels of the applicant pool. For this type of job, perhaps the interview should be primarily an RJP. For an organization with a bad reputation, PR may need to be a larger component of the interview. Interviewers should carefully consider what they are trying to accomplish within an individual interview and across the interview process.

Setting goals will provide a clear direction for interviewers as they develop and implement individual interviews. Setting goals can also help assure that the desired objectives are obtained across the interview process. Perhaps the easiest way to manage the interview process is to have Human Resources or senior management within the area coordinate interviewers. Prior to a candidate's visit, HR or senior management could facilitate a discussion among interviewers on who will focus on which goals. Interviewers need to agree where in the interview process the candidate will be measured, and where PR and RJP will occur. Alternatively, hiring managers could develop an agenda for the candidate's on-site visit and specify the goals of each interview. Then the agenda could be reviewed by HR or senior management. These facilitated discussions and reviews are designed to clearly specify goals, to identify and eliminate redundancies, and to make interviewers aware of what is actually happening in their selection process.

Strategy 2: Train and Motivate Interviewers to Conduct Accurate Measurement

Training and motivating interviewers to accurately measure whether a candidate can do the job is another important strategy for managing the interview process. Without the tools and motivation needed to identify good employees, interviewers will not accurately measure whether the candidate meets the organization's needs. As we have noted, managers often fail to measure candidates simply because they don't know how to do it effectively.

Accurate measurement can also contribute to achieving the other two potential interview goals—influencing the candidate by selling the positive features of the job and the organization and providing the information needed to help the candidate make a good job choice. Accurate measurement creates a positive, professional image of the organization since it sends the message that the organization knows what it wants and how to measure it. Research suggests that applicants seek out organizations that match their values.[9] High-quality employees look for organizations that demonstrate commitment to high quality in the way they assess their applicants.

In addition, the types of questions that lead to accurate measurement simultaneously communicate the requirements for the job and help the candidate assess whether the job is a good fit. Chapter Four describes some questioning techniques that provide accurate measurements of the candidate while they offer a preview of the job's requirements. Giving interviewers the training and motivation to accurately measure candidates is a critical strategy for managing the interview process.

Strategy 3: Manage a Unified PR Message

Accurate measurement can contribute to an enhanced PR image within an individual interview. However, accurate measurement cannot ensure that key messages (other than quality standards) that the organization wants to send will get through to new hires. Also, accurate measurement cannot ensure that a consistent message is provided. For example, one of the authors recently met with the college recruiting team of a large organization. The organization is family friendly with an open and supportive culture. When asked how this culture is conveyed in the interview, the team replied, "We just hope it comes across." This very well-managed organization is very conscious of its external image—but it has no management processes in place to make sure its desired message is sent to candidates.

Additionally, when ten interviewers from another organization were asked what they stressed about the benefits of the organization they worked for, seven different ideas were presented. All the interviewers agreed that the seven characteristics were reflective of their organization, but the interviewers each stressed what they valued the most and never addressed the others.

To present a unified PR message, the manager of the interviewing process needs to clearly define the image that the organization wants to create and the messages it intends to send—then clearly communicate the image and messages to all interviewers. Managing images and impressions with a unified approach will partially determine the kinds of candidates who are attracted to your organization as well as how the candidates will interact with you.

For a unified approach to PR:

1. Gather good data on the kind of information that candidates want before they accept an offer of employment. You can gather the information by anonymously surveying new hires shortly after their employment regarding what impressed them about the organization and led to their decision to join it. The survey must be clearly designed and grant anonymity for the respondents. New hires might be reluctant to openly express their views if they believe their responses will affect how others perceive them or their performance. (Exhibit 2.1 provides a sample recruiting assessment questionnaire.)
2. Use this data as part of interviewer training on PR. Once you understand what candidates typically want to know, you can design a message that will meet the information needs of your candidates. Target this message to the top quality

Exhibit 2.1. **Recruiting Assessment Questionnaire**
_____

This questionnaire is sent to all new hires one month after starting with our organization. The purpose of the questionnaire is to help us evaluate our recruiting efforts. Please be assured that your responses are anonymous. Please do not identify yourself anywhere on the questionnaire. Return it by mail and it will opened and analyzed by individuals who were not involved in hiring you. Your responses will be combined with the responses from others to assure confidentiality.

1. Please briefly describe any image or impressions that you developed about our organization based on how we recruited you. Please be specific. If you feel you received unclear messages or you received different messages from different individuals, please describe.

2. What, if any, of these messages or impressions influenced your decision to join us? Why and how did it influence you?

Exhibit 2.1. **Recruiting Assessment Questionnaire (cont.)**

3. Now that you have been employed, do you think we gave you an accurate picture of our organization?

   ☐ yes   ☐ no   ☐ somewhat

   If you did not answer yes to this question, please indicate how we could have been clearer or what should have been added.

4. What, if anything, has surprised and delighted you about working in our organization?

5. What didn't we tell you that we should have told you that would have been helpful in your decision whether to join our organization and to help you get off to an effective start on your job?

6. The following information is designed to help us categorize your responses to improve the way we recruit people like you. Again, please be assured that your individual responses will not be shared with the people who recruited you or to whom you report.

   _____ Department

   _____ Grade level

   _____ Functional area (Accounting, Human Resources, Sales, etc.)

candidates you are attempting to attract and hire. Each interviewer needs to know the messages the organization wants to send and how to contribute to a unified, positive image of the organization and the job.

3. Evaluate whether the organization's messages are accurately communicated. To attract and retain top quality employees, an organization needs not only to have the right message and image but also to convey it accurately. Evaluating the message that your new hires received during the interview process will help you determine whether your interviewers are really conveying the message you want them to convey.

These steps will not restrict management's ability to send the messages they believe should be sent about the job and the organization. Managers still have the discretion to provide specific information that is unique to their particular area. These steps will ensure, however, that applicants receive the desired common message that the organization wants to present.

Strategy 4: Evaluate Your RJPs

Providing truly realistic job previews should increase retention since candidates will self-select out of the hiring process if the organization does not meet their needs. Additionally, new hires should hit the ground running and be effective sooner since they will be aware of key hurdles. This initial success should create a "success breeds success" cycle.

Research on RJPs has not uniformly documented the glowing outcomes that were anticipated for their use. But one reason for the gap between intentions and results is the fact that RJPs do not always accurately convey the reality of the job.[10] As with PR, the judgment regarding what is "realistic" is often left to the interviewer. In addition, interviewers are typically not trained in effectively conveying the information, and rarely do interviewers get feedback about how well they conveyed the message. To make this process more effective, you must evaluate your realistic job previews to ensure that they are accurately reflecting the job and are clearly communicated. This information must be effectively summarized and fed back to interviewers to help them improve the effectiveness of their RJPs.

How can this be done? Organizations typically do exit interviews to determine why people leave. We are suggesting the addition of an "entrance assessment process" to improve the ability to attract and retain candidates. You can evaluate RJPs simply and inexpensively by sending anonymous questionnaires to new hires to assess whether the key realities have been described. Again, see Exhibit 2.1. You can modify the questions to suit your specific organizational needs. If your organization is large, you might reduce costs by distributing the questionnaire to just a sample of new recruits.

Strategy 5: Use Other Media for PR and RJP

One way to reduce some of the time devoted to PR and the RJP in the interviews is to use other media to communicate the information. This can be done by sending candidates information before the interview. Many organizations now have systems by which candidates can apply on-line. They provide PR information through their Web sites. Web sites also can be used to provide some preliminary RJP to allow candidates to do some initial screening of the organization. Certainly, the interviewer will still need to provide some PR and some RJP, but it will be more efficient to use the time primarily to clarify information that was sent via other sources.

Strategy 6: Evaluate the Effectiveness of Your Interviewing Process

One strategy to help the organization recognize the need for management of the interview process is to undertake a small pilot study to assess the extent to which the interview process is achieving its goals. At the end of the interview day, applicants can be asked to complete a short anonymous questionnaire about their opinions of the organization, their understanding of the job requirements, and their view of the interview process (for example, amount of redundancy and accuracy of measurement). They should be informed that their responses, which can be returned by mail, will be analyzed by someone not involved in the hiring decision and will be used only for measuring the effectiveness of the interview process. Exhibit 2.2 is an example of the type of questionnaire that could be used, although it should be adapted for the specific goals of the interview process.

The results from the questionnaires can create the baseline for assessing how your applicants perceive the strengths and weaknesses of your interviewing process. You can also determine the level of coordination that currently exists in the process. By monitoring this data over time, your organization can make adjustments to improve its effectiveness in selecting top quality candidates. Many organizations will be surprised when they discover how they are perceived by the people they are trying to hire.[11]

CHAPTER SUMMARY

In this chapter, we have described the first step in the Strategic Interviewing Approach—developing realistic goals to manage the interview process. We discussed the potential goals of interviewing and the problems that can occur when accurate measurement is squeezed out of the process, leaving managers to rely on general impressions for the hiring decision. We proposed a variety of strategies that manage the process while allowing managers the flexibility to address their needs. Strategies you can use for managing the interview process more effectively include setting clear goals for each interview, training and motivating managers to conduct accurate measurement, managing a unified PR message, evaluating your RJPs, and evaluating the effectiveness of your interviewing process.

Since the theme of this book is hiring good people, in the next four chapters, we will focus on how interviews can best be conducted for the

Exhibit 2.2. Interview Assessment Questionnaire

We would like your feedback about your interview(s) with our organization. We want your assessment of the day as a part of our continuing commitment to improve our selection process. Please do not identify yourself on this questionnaire. This questionnaire is anonymous and will have no impact on your hiring decision. No one involved in your hiring process will see your responses.

1. Overall, the interviews were an accurate assessment of my abilities to do the job that I was interviewed for.

   ☐ Strongly Agree   ☐ Agree   ☐ Neither Agree nor Disagree   ☐ Disagree   ☐ Strongly Disagree

   Please provide any information that would help us understand your answer.

2. Overall, I thought the organization showed me respect by making good use of my time.

   ☐ Strongly Agree   ☐ Agree   ☐ Neither Agree nor Disagree   ☐ Disagree   ☐ Strongly Disagree

   Please provide any information that would help us understand your answer.

3. I have a good understanding of the positive aspects of working for the organization.

   ☐ Strongly Agree   ☐ Agree   ☐ Neither Agree nor Disagree   ☐ Disagree   ☐ Strongly Disagree

   Please provide any information that would help us understand your answer.

4. I received a balanced view (the positive aspects and the challenges) of what it is like to work in the organization.

   ☐ Strongly Agree   ☐ Agree   ☐ Neither Agree nor Disagree   ☐ Disagree   ☐ Strongly Disagree

   Please provide any information that would help us understand your answer.

Please provide any other information about any aspect of your interaction with our organization that would help us understand your views.

Thank you for completing this questionnaire. Please return the questionnaire in the attached envelope.

goal of accurate measurement. Chapter Three describes how to define performance expectations, a critical step in accurately measuring and predicting whether the candidate will be a good employee.

The following "Perspectives" section demonstrates some of the many benefits of setting realistic goals and managing the interviewing process.

Perspectives on Interview Management

Mike Johnson, Human Resources Manager, Plante & Moran

Has this new way of interviewing had any impact on how your company is perceived and your ability to recruit? Also, how has it affected your ability to manage the limited time available for interviews?

I think that high-achieving people want to accomplish *getting* a job versus being given a job. They need to earn things that are important to them. I think if you don't do a good job of interviewing them, they feel slighted. So if you really want to get high-achievers, you need to make it difficult to some degree, otherwise they won't be interested. I think a lot of recruiters make it too easy for the top recruits and then they wonder why the candidates don't like them.

An example of this is reflected in a recent training program we conducted. We practiced interviews using both our old and new styles. We received unprompted testimonials from the candidates that our new style reflected much better on the company. They felt that the interviewer was really interested in them as opposed to being mean or hard to interview. I've also seen this approach help us attract top people that were initially interested in going to larger firms than us. As high-achieving people, they just assumed that is where they should be because that was the biggest firm for them to be in. Our interviewing style, our ability to communicate why we interview the way we do, what we are looking for and the connections between how we interview on campus to what we expect on the job, help them see that this is a place where they can thrive and have a lot of opportunities.

I have also seen this reflected in the last three years in terms of our numbers. We have had some very good years in very tough recruiting times. In each year we have hit our numbers while being able to increase quality. Using this approach, we have been able to attract a greater percentage of the higher-achieving people.

In terms of time, we have also seen benefits here. Having a strategy and clear questions—knowing why we are asking questions and what the answers should be—has given our recruiters more confidence in terms of making their decisions.

I also think the factors that they are using to make decisions are much better. I see that in their ability to describe why they want to hire someone. They are much more detailed and less likely to use a gut feeling as the basis for their decision. They are also providing us with the kind of information in their interview notes that lets us see why their decisions are appropriate. The quality is much better, which has given me more confidence that we are making the best use of our time but also making higher-quality decisions.

Susan J. Adams, Chief of Recruitment, International Monetary Fund

What impact, if any, has this new way of interviewing had on how your company is perceived and your ability to recruit? How has it affected your ability to manage the limited time available for interviews?

Several candidates have told me after the interview that their interview experiences with us were one of the best they have ever experienced. They saw consistency. They felt that the interview panelists were prepared and coordinated, and they felt they had a "fair try." They thought that the interview conveyed the standards of excellence that they perceived pervaded the entire organization. For example, one candidate told us, "If the interviewers are this professional, I can only imagine how competent my future colleagues on the line will be!"

Our revised interviewing approach has not necessarily resulted in any changes in our ability to recruit people, except that it has made the interviewing process more efficient on our side. We have systematized the process across candidates, and have saved time in making the final ranking of candidates.

This new interviewing approach has absolutely affected our ability to manage time better! We are interviewing more efficiently. And it has given our "left-brained" line managers the sense that we have a scientific approach to candidate selection.

Susan Mason, Vice President of Human Resources,
Old Kent Financial Services

What is the value of realistic job previews for Old Kent Financial Services?

The realistic job preview is a critical component of our interview process. We find that realistic job previews allow the interviewer to "sell" the candidate on the job, and provide the candidate with information required to make an appropriate decision should an offer be made.

In specific departments within the bank where we have focused on this goal, the longevity of the employees has been improved. One example is our Accelerated Career Track Program. New employees in this program have a good understanding of the job, its challenges, and its positive features because of our efforts to help them understand what it will be like to have this job.

Ideally, we would further reduce turnover and make better hiring decisions by consistently providing RJPs in our interviews.

Applications

1. What goals are you trying to achieve in your interviews?
2. How much time do you devote to measuring whether the candidate can do the job versus PR and the RJP in your interviews? What is your strategy for measuring whether the candidate can do the job?
3. What is your strategy for effectively presenting the image you want to present to candidates during the interview?
4. How do you present an RJP? Do you have evidence to validate that you are accurately presenting the key issues?
5. Do you coordinate and manage the PR, RJP, and assessment components of the interview?

Defining Performance Expectations

Predicting whether a candidate will meet your performance expectations on the job is the measurement objective for an interview. Essentially, you hire people on the belief that they will be good performers and that this will be reflected in future performance appraisals. Likewise, you reject applicants because you predict they won't be effective performers. Defining performance expectations is the first step to accurate measurement. If interviewers can't define what they want someone to do, they won't be able to accurately measure whether someone can perform effectively.

Chapter Two examined the importance of defining realistic goals and managing the interviewing process. This chapter tells how to achieve the goal of accurately measuring the candidate. First, it defines the three components of performance expectations for an interview. Then it explores two major problems in how they are used in interviews. Finally, it presents strategies for defining performance expectations.

■ Three Components of Performance Expectations

There are differences in the levels at which employees perform their jobs. Performance expectations are the standards an interviewer uses to determine the expected level of performance for an employee. For the purpose of preparing an interview, the three components of performance expectations are goals, job barriers, and competency requirements. Each of these components is described in the following sections.

Goals

In every job employees are expected to achieve goals. A goal is an end result that produces a direct, positive benefit to the organization. Goals are a part of performance expectations and should be assessed through the interview process since you want to hire people who will achieve the desired results. For example, if you are hiring a salesperson and your expectations involve reaching a certain sales quota, you are trying to predict through the interview if the new hire will reach the goal. You might interview differently if the sales quota you expect from the new hire is $50 million in sales than if the quota is $1 million. Your performance expectation will influence what you ask and what you look for in the new hire. Keep in mind that goals are only one part of performance expectations that you need to measure.

Job Barriers

Job barriers are the second component of performance expectations. Job barriers are key job situations an employee has to overcome in order to be an effective performer (a "good employee") and achieve important organizational goals. Think about the last performance appraisal you gave an employee. Did you actually base your ratings of the employee on everything that the employee did on the job? If you are like most managers, you used certain events that the employee handled or failed to handle appropriately on the job as the basis for your rating. These events or situations are the job barriers. The job analysis technique for identifying the job barriers is a modification of the critical incident approach.[1] Most contemporary approaches to interviewing use some variation of this approach.[2]

Think back to our salesperson example. What if you were interviewing a candidate who has a history of making sales that far exceeded your expected sales quota? Would you hire the applicant? Many interviewers would jump at this type of candidate and say, "Yes, of course!" Others would want to know more. The interviewer who wants more information might have concerns about the candidate's previous experiences. Behind the concern would be a need to verify that the salesperson with the history of high sales had demonstrated the ability to overcome the same kinds of challenges that will come up in the new job.

Competency Requirements

Competency requirements are the third component of performance expectations. Competency requirements describe how you would like your employees to behave in job barrier situations. Returning to our salesperson example, what if you found that the person with the history of high sales had already worked in your industry and faced many of the same challenges meeting their sales quotas? Would you hire this candidate? Again, some people immediately say, "Yes, of course!" Others still want to know more. Those who want more information might have concerns about how the barriers were overcome. Did the salesperson use high-pressure sales techniques? Were unrealistic promises made? Was there any unethical behavior? Or did the salesperson show a creative ability to identify the customer's true need? Was the person able to explain the range of options available on the product and how those might apply to different needs? Indicating how you expect the person to act or not act in important job situations defines competency requirements.

Does this mean that interviewers who immediately hire the candidate do not have competency requirements? No, it probably means the interviewers simply have not specified their competency requirements. Have you ever hired anyone who, on paper, had all the appropriate experiences and even a history of getting results—but once hired achieved results in a way that caused problems and led to poor performance? If you think back to the way you interviewed that person, you probably focused heavily on the goals and job barriers components of your performance expectation, but failed to specify the competency requirements—how job barriers should be addressed.

There is a difference between competency requirements and competencies. As we have noted, competency requirements describe how you expect someone to perform in job barrier situations. The standards you set for the job performance you expect will determine the competency requirements. There is no one universally accepted definition of a competency; however, competencies are typically thought of as characteristics of individuals and the combination of the knowledge, skills, abilities, attitudes, and values that they possess that apply in a variety of situations.

In many organizations today, interviewers focus on assessing the applicant's competencies.[3] Although an individual's competencies are clearly important, focusing solely on competencies can be misguided. Interviewers may concentrate on determining the candidate's competencies without giving sufficient attention to whether the competencies will produce the desired results and overcome job barriers. In other words, interviewers often focus on what the candidate has without appropriately defining whether it is what is needed to meet performance expectations. Applicants may have numerous competencies, but interviewers have to determine if the competencies are relevant for the job.

Additionally, interviewers must determine if a specific competency will apply to the range of situations that exist in their organization. Consider an entry-level job in your organization that many employees perform and many managers supervise. Does one supervisor expect a job barrier to be handled in a particular way and another supervisor expect it to be handled in a radically different and almost opposite manner? Is it realistic to expect that the same set of behaviors are needed to meet the expectations of both supervisors?

Certainly there are some competencies that apply across various situations. Almost every organization today needs what it calls "team players." Yet employees rated as good team players in one organization might be rated poor team players in another organization because there are different expectations for being a team player. Thus, a candidate could have the *team player competency* but would not always match the *team player competency requirements* of the job in question.

Throughout this book we use the term *competency requirements* when we are referring to the performance expectations for the job. We use the term *competency* when we are referring to characteristics of individuals who may be talented but not necessarily able to meet specific performance expectations. Focusing on competency requirements leads to more precise measurement of good employees. In Chapter Four, we will develop this point further when we discuss the link between performance expectations and questions.

■ Problems in Defining Performance Expectations

Whoever will be hiring the candidate should know the basis for the final decision before they begin interviewing candidates. Intuitively, this starting point may make sense, but many managers and HR professionals fail to define their expectations or do it poorly. In the following section we outline why these problems exist and the consequences they have for accurate measurement.

Gathering Too Little Job Information

Who is better able to define what should get done on a job than the person who will eventually assess the performance? One of the keys to developing more effective interviews is to start by having the new hire's direct manager define the performance expectations for the open position.

However, many managers begin the process of looking for a new employee by immediately shifting to what they think is the solution to their problem. These managers describe their needs in terms of what they want the candidate to be ("I want a good team player") rather than what they want the candidate to do ("I want someone who can get a team that has had a history of conflict to work together to achieve their goals").

In this example, it appears that the supervisor is specifying a competency requirement, "team player," but earlier we described a competency requirement as how an employee should act to overcome a job barrier. In the "team player" example there is no description of how the person should behave, nor are the job barriers defined. Why a team player is required is not clear. The words are a label that could have multiple meanings.

Ask ten managers to define *team player* and see how many different answers you get. In a recent interviewing seminar, we asked human resource professionals and hiring managers that question. Exhibit 3.1 lists some of their answers.

Each definition is appropriate for describing a team player in a particular situation. However, determining which, if any, of these definitions—or what combination of them—is best for the current situation is impossible without knowing more about the job barriers that need to be addressed. Interviewers need to understand why they want to hire a "team player" and how they want that person to behave. Without defining the job barriers and competency requirements, they are unlikely to accurately measure their performance expectations during the interview.

Sometimes interviewers partially define their performance expectations. This can occur if someone is hired for the results they have produced in the past without much consideration for the job barriers they had to overcome or the processes they used to get there. An interviewer who accepts a candidate solely on results has either consciously or unconsciously assumed that the candidate can handle the job barriers needed for success in the new job.

Exhibit 3.1. Various Managers' Descriptions of a "Team Player"

- Sacrifices for the good of the team
- Gets everyone moving in the same direction
- Someone who can motivate others
- A good listener who understands others' perspectives
- Does whatever needs to get done to reach the goal
- Someone who can perform a range of important activities
- Goes along with the team's decision, even if he doesn't like it, because it is best for the team
- Handles conflict in a positive manner

The following example illustrates how this assumption can be misleading. A midsized company was interested in hiring a new director of safety. Because the company wanted to improve its own safety record, it searched for and hired an employee who had a history of keeping workers accident-free. After being hired, the employee failed to meet the performance expectations for the job. The employee failed because the company had a poor safety history and many people were resistant to change. The new employee had never had to face these barriers before. Likewise, the employee was unable to reduce the organization's resistance to change and improve its approach to safety. The employee had a strong history of results, but those results were achieved in companies that had strong commitments to safety. This person had what was needed to maintain a safety program but not to get one started in an environment with strong resistance to change.

Gathering Too Much Job Information

Some managers recognize the need to develop their interview process by focusing on the job and identifying performance expectations. Because of their experience supervising employees who have the job they are trying to fill, managers have considerable expertise determining performance expectations. These managers often provide numerous details on duties and responsibilities. In fact, the level of detail far exceeds what can possibly be assessed in a typical interview.

Think of all the different things you do on your job. Is it possible to ask you about all of those activities in the typical thirty- to sixty-minute interview? Managers in technical jobs are often skeptical that other interviewers can evaluate someone from their functional area. They believe that an interviewer could not possibly know all the technical situations that an employee might face.

Managers who raise this concern are partially correct. Interviewers can't know all aspects of another person's job. However, what many managers don't understand is that there is no need to know all aspects of the job. Many performance expectations are quite similar when you focus on what needs to be accomplished and the competency requirements needed to achieve it. Additionally, there are some performance expectations that don't differentiate between workers' effectiveness.

An example of a performance expectation that would usually not differentiate among workers is completing routine paperwork. Often good and poor workers complete routine paperwork. Why focus on the ability to handle this type of situation, when the competency requirement does not separate the effective from the ineffective worker? Instead, managers need to identify and focus on key performance expectations that differentiate workers. They need a process to help them do this.

Continuing with this logic, managers also need to have processes for linking questions and answers to performance expectations. Chapter Four will address this issue. For now, we turn to a discussion of the process that can be used to define performance expectations.

■ Strategies for Developing Performance Expectations

In this section, we explain the way a new employee's immediate supervisor should approach the task of developing performance expectations. We clarify each of the performance expectation components (goals, job barriers, and competency requirements) by discussing strategies for defining them.

Before you read the rest of the chapter, take a minute to answer these questions by completing Assessment 3.1 about any job for which you are the hiring manager. If you do not hire employees, use your own job or one for which you have a clear

■ Assessment 3.1. ■		
Defining Developing Performance Expectations		
What are the important job goals?	What are the situations (job barriers) that must be overcome to achieve the goals?	How should the situations be handled? What actions (competency requirements) would demonstrate an effective or ineffective performer?

understanding of the performance expectations. We will refer to this list later in this chapter.

Strategy 1: Define the Goals

To be useful as performance expectations, goals should be specific and measurable. The goal that salespeople "have a good relationship with their clients" is neither. How would a manager evaluate whether a salesperson has met the goal? If a goal is specific and measurable, there should not be any disagreement about whether a person met or did not meet the goal. The indicators of success or failure are clear and observable by others.

An example of a specific and measurable goal might be to receive a sale from a customer without having it go through a competitive bidding process. This could be your expectation of what it means to "have a good relationship" with a client. Take a look at the goals you listed in Assessment 3.1. Are they specific and measurable? Would you and someone else be likely to agree that a job incumbent reached or missed these goals? If your goals are not specific and measurable, you will not be able to accurately measure them through an interview process.

Strategic interviewers acknowledge that similar jobs may have different expectations and different goals. For example, two supervisors may perform similar tasks but have different performance expectations if the goal for one supervisor is to improve the quality of work while the goal for the other supervisor is to increase the amount of work produced.

Similarly, two jobs may have the same goals but different job barriers that must be addressed. You may be hiring two supervisors, both of whom you expect to improve the quality of their subordinates' work. However, if one will have to work with a group of highly technical workers who have had a history of conflict while the other will have to work with relatively unskilled workers who are highly cohesive, the job barriers would not be the same. And even when the goals and job barriers are the same for a particular job, there may be differences in how new employees are expected to address the barriers. Once goals are defined, the job barriers can be used to determine what needs to get done and the competency requirements can indicate how it should be done to attain the desired goals.

Strategy 2: Define the Job Barriers

In Assessment 3.1, did you start defining job barriers by asking yourself, "What is it that people do on this job?" If so, you probably listed numerous tasks, many of which will not differentiate performance among employees. Instead, the question should be "What are the types of situations that good performers handle in one way, while poor performers handle in a different way?" For example, processing the typical refund request would not be a job barrier for a clerk position, if it is something that good and poor performers do equally effectively. However, processing this type of request for an extremely angry customer who has lost the sales receipt might be, if it is something that differentiates the clerks' performance.

If you are like most of us, you probably had some difficulty in listing the job barriers in Assessment 3.1. Part of the reason for this is that we typically don't think of why we like or dislike something, we just know that we do. You probably are not aware of your standards. The following tactics can help you develop the job barriers component of your performance expectations:

1. *Identify people who are meeting or failing to meet key performance expectations.* Then focus on the critical job-related situations that led to this assessment. Apply this tactic to the job you used in Assessment 3.1. Can you think of someone who is very good at this job? What are the situations that make this employee stand out from others in terms of performance? Ask the same questions for people that you feel do not meet your expectations.

2. *Identify successful or unsuccessful new employees and isolate the situations that lead to your assessment.* Again, focus on the job you used in Assessment 3.1. Have you ever worked with someone who after just a short time in the position you knew would be very successful or unsuccessful? What were the situations they handled that led you to your prediction of success or failure?

3. *Work backwards from labels of desired competencies.* Think of someone who would be ideal for the job you described in Assessment 3.1. What do they do that leads to success? If you are like most of us, you will apply a label to describe this behavior. You might say, for example, that the person is "a leader," or is "organized." Now ask yourself, "What situations does the person handle to qualify as a leader, or as organized?" In a sense what you are doing is backing into the

job barrier from the label for the competency requirement describing how the person should behave.

The barriers you listed should not be unique requirements of your organization's practices or procedures. They are situations that someone should know how to handle as a function of their expertise—expected behaviors they can demonstrate without targeted on-the-job training. For example, you will not want to define pricing the cost of a project as a job barrier if your company's methodology is not commonly used. Instead, a relevant job barrier might be handling a report with numbers that are not internally consistent. The competency requirements in this situation are the actions the employee takes to resolve the inconsistency. We would expect new employees in this position to know how to check the accuracy of reports but not how to use the company's pricing methodology.

While the process of developing job barriers may seem time-consuming at first, you do not really need a large number of barriers to create an effective interview. You are not trying to identify all the barriers that reflect all the different tasks that individuals perform on a job. Remember, your focus is on the things that separate the effective from the ineffective performer.

Strategy 3: Define the Competency Requirements

As you look at your job barriers in Assessment 3.1, do you see that there is clearly a set of right and wrong actions or behaviors that should be taken in each situation? These are the competency requirements that describe how you want things done. If you have a hard time listing the competency requirements, you may have a poor example of a job barrier. Perhaps the job barrier doesn't distinguish between effective and ineffective workers. Another possibility is that you may not have clearly defined how you expect work to be done.

This was illustrated in a recent training session where an information systems supervisor of a large organization identified a job barrier as a team project that was past the deadline. When asked for the right set of behaviors, the supervisor said that a good worker should "lead." The wrong behavior was "fail to lead." Despite considerable prompting, the supervisor could never really define what should or should not be done in the situation. This is an example of a supervisor who hasn't really defined the competency requirement component of this performance expectation.

The Strategic Interviewing Approach does not dictate the performance standards managers should use to assess candidates. Managers can set the standard at whatever level they believe is appropriate. However, standards must exist before anyone can accurately measure whether a candidate can meet them. The Strategic Interviewing Approach does provide the process for managers to understand and define their performance standards by clarifying performance expectations.

After you have defined job barriers handled by an effective performer, you can clarify the competency requirements by asking, "What actions should the person take in this situation?" In some cases, hiring managers will not describe the actions the person should take. Instead, they will emphasize the expected results. Other hiring managers may give specific examples of how they expect workers to behave.

Consider two managers, both looking for administrative assistants. Both managers have the same performance expectation—their assistants will handle customer complaints called into the office. The first manager outlines a specific set of expectations describing how the candidate should behave in this situation. For example, the first manager may expect the administrative assistant to listen to the customer's complaint, diagnose the root cause, and find a resolution that satisfies the customer and sends the message that the organization values each customer. The second manager only expresses an interest in results—a satisfied customer. The interviewer who is developing the competency requirements should ask the second manager whether the administrative assistant needs to satisfy the customer in a particular manner. If not, the ability to satisfy the customer is the competency requirement that the second manager expects.

Some managers may not care how a situation is resolved as long as it is. These managers, when pressed, will list the end result or goal as the desired action because they haven't really thought through their expectations. How an employee handles a situation is often the key differentiation in performance. Thus, to identify good employees, you need to describe the competency requirements as specifically as possible. Competency requirements that are well defined contain observable actions and behaviors, outline the context in which the actions are performed, and describe observable results of actions.

The following tactics are helpful in developing competency requirements:

- Include action verbs such as *solves, generates, proposes,* or *originates.* Action verbs describe behavior—and behavior can be measured.
- Ask what behaviors are needed to handle each job barrier. Describe how someone has acted in the situation that met or failed to meet your performance expectations.
- Ask yourself whether another observer could easily recognize the presence or absence of the competency requirement. If you are the only one that can recognize it, chances are the competency requirement has not been behaviorally defined since you rely on your intuition to measure it.
- Put it in writing. Describe what you are looking for in words.
- Avoid using ambiguous or subjective verbs such as *understands, feels,* or *believes.* You can't measure whether someone

understands, feels, or believes something. If it is not measurable, it is not useful as a criterion for assessing a job applicant.

- Ask yourself what recommendations you would give to an employee who performed poorly in the job barrier situation. What feedback would you give that person? What would you tell that person to do differently?

Don't be discouraged if your competency requirements do not meet all of the points noted here. Keep in mind that developing job barriers and competency requirements is a skill that develops with practice. Table 3.1 lists some typical job barriers and corresponding competency requirements.

Job barriers and competency requirements explain differences in performance appraisals among workers with the same job. As a result, they provide important information for the hir-

Table 3.1. Job Barriers and Corresponding Competency Requirements

Job Barriers	Corresponding Competency Requirements
The work cannot be completed before the end of the work day.	Identifying in sufficient time that the work cannot be completed and developing and implementing a plan that meets deadlines and work specifications.
A client is dissatisfied and expresses an intention to switch business to another company.	Recognizing the client is dissatisfied and taking action to identify and correct the cause of the client's concerns before the client switches business to another company.
Everything is going fine at work.	Taking action to make an effective process even better.
The employee encounters a problem on a project or assignment in an area outside the scope of prior training.	Independently seeking out and finding solutions beyond those indicated by specific training.

ing process. Would you give a high performance appraisal rating to someone who did an effective job of handling the job barriers you listed in Assessment 3.1? If not, you are either missing some job barriers or have listed some that really aren't important to the job.

Strategy 4: Address the Challenges in Defining Performance Expectations

As with any methodology, challenges will arise in applying the process. One challenge that interviewers mention is applying this process to a new position. They often ask, "How can I define job barriers when I can't observe good and bad performers in the job?" To answer this question, you have to ask the hiring manager or people in comparable positions to define the key situations that they want handled and how those situations should be addressed. New positions are developed to meet specific needs. Job barriers should help define those needs by specifying the situations that must be handled to demonstrate effectiveness.

A second challenge is that managers may have unrecognized or unarticulated standards. One strategy to meet this challenge is having hiring managers review completed performance appraisals for the position they are attempting to fill. Managers need to review why there are differences in ratings. They need to examine the factors that influenced the appraisal decisions and include those situations in the selection process. If the previous job incumbent handled an important situation on the job in a way that dissatisfied the manager, the manager needs to assess how the next incumbent should handle it.

Another strategy for developing performance expectations is to ask for job barriers from the job incumbent as part of the exit interview process. Ask the person to describe key situations that demonstrated either successes or failures on the job. By this process, hiring managers can gain insight into performance standards that they may have overlooked. Similarly, examining training programs or developmental plans can also provide insight into the types of situations that differentiate employees.

A third challenge in applying the performance expectations methodology involves the manager who focuses too much on short-term goals when describing performance expectations. When positions are open, managers tend to concentrate on their immediate needs. A related but slightly different concern is that jobs may change too quickly for definitive performance standards. While it is true that jobs are changing at a rapid rate, employees will be hired to do *something.* Managers still need to define what that something is and what level of performance they expect. Today, many jobs have the job barrier of dealing with a rapidly changing environment or changing job requirements. However, not all hiring managers have the same expectations of how this barrier should be addressed. To provide the most accurate measurement, managers need to define their competency requirements for this type of situation.

■ The Role of the Human Resource Professional

To this point, we have been focusing on the process of determining performance expectations. We have suggested that hiring managers are the best source of performance expectations. What role should the Human Resource professional play in the process of defining what needs to get done and how to accomplish it? Perhaps the biggest contribution is to challenge the assumption that managers will necessarily know the performance expectations they want the candidate to meet or exceed. The more an HR professional can push hiring managers into the areas where they can make the greatest contribution, such as defining the situations they want handled, the greater the connection between the job, the performance expectations, and the question-and-answer process.

HR professionals can also make an important contribution by not accepting the use of labels to define competency requirements and by assisting managers to define terms behaviorally. We will discuss ways to accomplish this in more detail in Chapter Six. For now, the point is that HR professionals involved in the interviewing process need to recognize that they are not "order takers" who simply gather information from knowledgeable supervisors. HR professionals should be familiar with the strategies and techniques that can be used to conduct better interviews. They should also view themselves as facilitators of the process and champions of quality standards for the interview process within their organization.

■ Performance Expectations for Technical Employees

Identifying technical performance expectations is important when you are hiring technical employees. Here is an example from a large multinational organization that was selecting information systems professionals. The managers began identifying job barriers by asking, "What are the types of situations that information systems professionals have to face?" and "What determines their effectiveness, regardless of the unique position that they hold within the company?" These questions led them to develop a list of job barriers that cut across jobs, including these seven:

- Technical and nontechnical people are confused about the basis for a specific recommendation.
- A customer or user has an unrealistic request or one that is not appropriate for his or her needs.

- A team disagrees internally about the correct strategy to address a pressing problem.
- The IS professional has to deal with computer code in an area in which he or she has not been trained to solve a problem.
- The IS professional must kick off a project.
- The IS professional made a mistake.
- The customer or user is unhappy or is dissatisfied with the IS professional's work.

These seven job barriers did not address all the situations that had to be handled in all the information systems positions. Still, most people agreed that all IS individuals needed to be able to address these job barriers. The next challenge was defining the competency requirements that matched the performance standards for these situations. Since these situations cut across all IS jobs, they were defined as core competency requirements. Think of core competency requirements as forming the base of a triangle—the solid foundation of every effective performer. The top area of the triangle includes the specific technical and interpersonal competency requirements needed for a particular position.

Looking at the types of situations the managers in this example thought were the job barriers, some people are mistakenly led to believe that this technique is only appropriate for "soft skills," including interpersonal or leadership competencies. However, this approach applies equally well to job-specific technical assessment. To use the approach effectively, you have to be able to define what it means to be technically competent. Knowing facts about technology or a discipline is not enough since someone could know the facts and not know when or how to apply them.

Technical competence involves recognizing what needs to be done in a particular situation and how it should be accomplished. Instead of starting by saying, "I want someone to know a specific piece of information" (a technical fact), you should start by asking what you want accomplished. Do you expect the person to reach a specific goal? Or do you expect a particular situation to be handled in a particular way? In the interview, you can assess whether the candidate knows what needs to be done in the situation and how to do it. Also, you can determine if the applicant can produce results. This assessment will lead to an accurate measurement of the person's technical competency that meets your requirements.

■ Additional Benefits of Clearly
Defined Performance Expectations

The process we have described in this chapter is designed to improve the interview process, but it has other important benefits in human resource management. More clearly defining what needs to get done and how the work should be accomplished should lead to the following benefits:

- *More effective delegation.* Delegation is a process of selecting people from a very limited pool (current job incumbents) to perform a task. When a manager delegates work to someone, that manager is predicting that the employee will meet performance expectations, just as we do in the hiring process. The more clearly we know what we are looking for someone to do and how we want it done, the easier it will be to choose the right person for the right tasks.
- *Better performance appraisals.* Since we have focused on connecting the performance appraisal process to the interview, both processes should be improved. Managers will know what to look for and will be sending a consistent message to employees about performance standards.
- *Enhanced training and development.* One of the challenges in providing people with good training is knowing what you

should be training them to do. This process helps to define what the employee needs to do by clarifying goals, job barriers, and competency requirements. As a result, there should be a stronger connection between job requirements and training.

- *More effective coaching and counseling.* To be good coaches and counselors, managers need to know not only what they want people to do but how they want them to do it. This process provides managers with strategies for clearly defining goals, job barriers, and competency requirements to meet performance standards.

Overall, the process of defining performance expectations helps people be better managers, and better management will attract better employees. While the job acceptance decision is complex and is influenced by various factors, an applicant's decision to reject a job can be heavily influenced by one particular concern: "Will I be successful in this organization?" Skilled people want to go to a place where they have the opportunity to be successful. Organizations that are better at selecting, assessing performance, training, and coaching and counseling provide an environment that is more likely to lead to success—and applicants are aware of the difference.

CHAPTER SUMMARY

An interview is an attempt to predict whether a candidate will meet or exceed your performance expectations on the job. In Chapter Three we began by defining the three components of performance expectations: goals, job barriers, and competency requirements. We also discussed the typical problems that occur when interviewers prepare for an interview by gathering either too little or too much job information.

The strategies presented in Chapter Three help you develop performance expectations so you can predict if the applicant will be an employee that adds value to your organization. Key strategies include: define the goals you expect employees to achieve; define the job barriers that typically block employees from attaining their goals; define the competency requirements, which are the employees' actions that demonstrate they can overcome the job barriers and attain the goals in the desired manner; and address the challenges in defining performance expectations.

We also discussed the role of the human resource professional in challenging hiring managers to define the behaviors they expect employees to demonstrate. With clear performance expectations, you will be ready for the next step, developing questions and identifying the answers that will help you to assess whether the applicant will or will not meet your performance expectations. Chapter Four will address this next step in the interview process.

The following "Perspectives" illustrate the positive impact of well-defined performance expectations on the interviewing process. They also highlight the importance of connecting the interview process to other aspects of performance management.

Perspectives on Performance Expectations

Mike Johnson, Human Resources Manager, Plante & Moran

Do you see any differences in the performance expectations that interviewers use to develop their interviews? Has this had any impact on other aspects of your performance management process?

Our performance system uses the same competencies that people use in campus recruiting. So the people who do interviewing use the same standards that new hires will face when they become employed. This wasn't always the case. Now, our interviewing objectives are tied in with our performance objectives.

I haven't seen the reversal of our interviews driving our performance management process, but perhaps some of that is because we have them already well connected. However, in the future, I see the possibility of using input from our campus recruiters to reassess our performance objectives. The recruiters know the supply out there since they are on the front lines. The stuff we are looking for may just not be there. So we may have to change our strategy and adjust based on the input from our college recruiters.

Susan J. Adams, Chief of Recruitment, International Monetary Fund

Do you see any differences in the performance expectations that interviewers use to develop their interviews? Has this had any impact on other aspects of your performance management process?

By defining, before the interview, the appropriate and insufficient answer ranges, we have a much better sense of "benchmarking" candidates throughout the interviews, and this makes the scoring of answers more accurate. It also enables the interviewers to listen for specific language in the answers.

In one recent interview, we used the benchmarks developed for the interviews to determine the skills gaps in the selected candidate, which in turn led to the proposal for a first-year training plan for the new candidate on the job.

Susan Mason, Vice President of Human Resources,
Old Kent Financial Services

Please provide some examples of the performance expectations you have set since you began using the Strategic Interviewing Approach. How is this different from what you were looking for previously?

When we created a new Interviewer Guide for Old Kent's Accelerated Career Track Program, we included our newly defined performance expectations. Previously, we put a lot of weight on cultural fit and the industrial psychologist's evaluation. Today, we focus on specific behaviors such as leadership potential, management style, communication skills, and proven project management examples.

Applications

1. When you search for a new employee, how do you determine what the employee needs to be able to do?
2. How do you determine the types of situations that good performers handle in one way while poor performers handle in a different way?
3. What job behaviors do you look for as a sign that a newly hired employee will meet your performance expectations?
4. How do you use your performance expectations in coaching, delegating and conducting performance appraisals?

4

Developing Job-Related Questions and Answers

What assumptions do you make when you ask a candidate questions in an interview? Many interviewers have not given this issue much thought. This chapter will explore the faulty assumptions that lead to ineffective interviewing questions and present strategies for developing questions and answers that effectively discover whether the candidate can meet or exceed performance expectations. It will also discuss ways to protect your organization against complaints alleging discrimination.

Before we begin our discussion of questions, it's useful to examine what can happen in an interview when interviewers assume that because they are good conversationalists, they are also good at asking questions in an interview.

■ Interviewer Traps

If the interviewer says "Tell me about yourself," the candidate may reveal a major flaw that indicates he or she is unqualified for the position. The question traps the candidate, who naively provides important revealing information—but it also traps the interviewer into thinking that the question is an effective measure of job-related competencies. What the interviewer fails to see is that this "revelation" says more about the candidate's ignorance of the interview process than about the interviewer's knowledge of it. The interviewer mistakenly takes this revelation as a sign of skill in getting a keen insight into the character of would-be employees.[1]

Interviewers can also be trapped by a "professional interviewee." This is the candidate who lacks the skills for the job but has developed an understanding of how to manipulate impressions in the interview.[2] In the interview, the candidate may give an overinflated view of the strengths for the job. The interviewer is then completely surprised when the candidate that looked so perfect fails to meet the performance expectations.

Professional interviewees gain several advantages by taking control of the interview.[3] First, these candidates give the impression that they are interested in the job and care about the organization. Second, these candidates can create an impression of being prepared and knowledgeable workers. If the candidates research the company and ask specific questions about the job and the organization, some interviewers conclude that these applicants are highly qualified and motivated for the open positions. Although preparation does suggest the candidates know how to prepare for the interview process, it doesn't necessarily indicate anything about how these professional interviewees prepare for job-related tasks. Third, and perhaps most important, too many questions from the candidate reduce the time for measuring whether the applicant can meet performance expectations. With less time for measurement, there is less chance either to gather accurate data or to expose flaws.

As you complete Assessment 4.1, mark the sample interview questions as effective or ineffective. Consider whether you are likely to gather accurate information or to expose flaws. Also give your rationale for each response. We will come back to your responses later in this chapter.

■ Faulty Assumptions Leading to Ineffective Interviewing Questions

Ineffective interviewing questions are those that typically do not lead to information necessary for assessing whether the candidate can meet the job's performance expectations. If useful information is obtained from ineffective questions, that usually results from chance or the lack of expertise or sophistication of the candidate, rather than from the capacity of the questions to accurately measure the desired performance expectations. An expert candidate—in the sense of being a professional interviewee—can answer ineffective interviewing questions in a way that leads an interviewer to mistakenly think the candidate is right for the job.

Effective interviewing questions allow you to gather information about the candidate's ability to meet your performance expectations, but they do not rely on the candidate's level of expertise or sophistication with the interview process to be effective. Even the most professional interviewee has a difficult time

---

■ Assessment 4.1. ■
Are These Effective or Ineffective Questions?

---

1. Tell me about a time when you were a member of a team and what your role was on the team.

   ☐ Effective Question   ☐ Ineffective Question

   Rationale:

2. If I asked your most recent supervisor to describe you, what would he or she say?

   ☐ Effective Question   ☐ Ineffective Question

   Rationale:

3. Why are you the best candidate for this job?

   ☐ Effective Question   ☐ Ineffective Question

   Rationale:

4. Give me an example of a situation when you set priorities on the job. Tell me why you set them as you did.

   ☐ Effective Question   ☐ Ineffective Question

   Rationale:

5. Have you ever had more work than could be finished by the deadline? What did you do?

   ☐ Effective Question   ☐ Ineffective Question

   Rationale:

■ **Assessment 4.1.** ■

Are These Effective or Ineffective Questions? (cont.)

---

6. Tell me about a situation in which you disagreed with your boss on handling an important issue. What did you do? Why?

   ☐ Effective Question   ☐ Ineffective Question

   Rationale:

7. Describe the most difficult problem you have faced on your previous job.

   ☐ Effective Question   ☐ Ineffective Question

   Rationale:

8. What is your greatest accomplishment?

   ☐ Effective Question   ☐ Ineffective Question

   Rationale:

9. Describe a situation in which you applied your education or some knowledge learned from a different job to improve a new situation. What did you do and how did it improve the situation?

   ☐ Effective Question   ☐ Ineffective Question

   Rationale:

10. Why did you select the college you attended?

    ☐ Effective Question   ☐ Ineffective Question

    Rationale:

responding persuasively to effective interviewing questions without being qualified for the job.

Interview questions are based on two types of assumptions. Some assumptions relate to the accuracy of measurement, others to the connection between what is measured and what is required for the job.[4] Unfortunately, interviewers usually don't think about their assumptions—and when the assumptions are faulty, the results are ineffective questions and interviews. Ineffective questions and ineffective interviews fail to connect what is measured to what is expected on the job. As you read about the following faulty assumptions, ask yourself to what extent they apply to your ratings of the questions in Assessment 4.1.

Assuming That Interviewees Accurately Describe Their Competencies

Candidates will not necessarily accurately describe their competencies. When interviewers ask, "What are your weaknesses?" it's unlikely that a candidate will answer, "My weakness is that I steal," or "I verbally abuse my subordinates." The professional interviewee has a finely tuned strategy of turning a weakness into a strength. Typical responses might include "I am a workaholic" or "I care too much about quality." A cartoon provides one of the best responses to the question about weaknesses. The cartoon character responds, "I lie during interviews."

Even if the candidate is being truthful, the answer may not reflect reality. Think of friends or colleagues whose self-perceptions do not reflect their true strengths. Why should we assume that people truly know their strengths or weaknesses and are willing to accurately describe them?

Even if candidates do describe their actual strengths or weaknesses, the interviewer has no basis to assess the standards that the candidates are using to make the assessment. The weakness of a professional athlete may be a strength for someone else. Essentially, the interviewer is asking candidates to assume the role of psychologist and analyze themselves.[5] There is no evidence to support the ability of interviewees to analyze themselves and the value of asking them to do so is doubtful.[6]

Assuming That Questions Do Not Need to Have Clear Right and Wrong Answers

Many interviewers believe there is a no need for a clear set of right and wrong answers to the interview questions they ask. "Who are your role models?" is the type of question with no real right or wrong answer. Who are the wrong role models? More important, what do candidates' answers say about their ability to perform on the job? Certainly, a very unsophisticated candidate might give an extreme response like "Napoleon" or "Marie Antoinette," but the candidate will more likely name someone the interviewer does not know. As a result, the candidate's answer is neither right nor wrong, and the interviewer cannot use it to measure the applicant against the performance expectations for the job.

The problem is that interviewers are often more focused on the questions than on the answers. As a result, they do not realize that the possible answers are often contradictory. Suppose an interviewer wants to measure a candidate's motivation. The interviewer asks, "Where do you want to be five years from now?" One candidate answers, "I plan to be a vice president." A second candidate answers, "I'm not sure. I want to be in a position where I am continuing to learn."

For those interviewers who are trying to measure the applicant's motivation through this question, an answer that indicates high goals ("I plan to be a vice president") is viewed as a good answer. The wrong answer is a response that shows some uncertainty or a lack of clear focus ("I am willing to contribute in any type of job that is enjoyable"). Unfortunately, this question does not necessarily measure motivation. Someone could aspire to be a vice president without being willing to put the effort into job performance. Some interviewers might use this same question to assess if the job "fits" the candidate's career goals. In this case, the high-aspiration answer, previously viewed as a good answer, now becomes a poor answer, since the chance of making vice president in five years is remote. The uncertain answer and the answer that reflects a willingness to contribute to any type of job, previously viewed as poor answers, now become right answers. Questions such as this one, measuring two different things to which answers can be right or wrong depending on the interviewer's purpose, do not provide valid information for making good hiring decisions.

Assuming That the Applicant's Experience Demonstrates Competency

Managers probably recognize the fallacy in the assumption that having experience in a particular area means someone has developed a competency in that area. Unfortunately, many managers operate as though this assumption were true when they ask questions like "Have you had experience supervising workers?" or "How many programs have you written in C++?" The fallacy lies in assuming that a person who has had certain experiences has necessarily developed certain skills. We all know people who have had considerable experience yet continue to make the same mistakes.

One reason that interviewers make this assumption is that experience is easy to measure; you either have experience or you don't have experience. Untrained interviewers are often unsure how to define and measure performance, so they measure experience instead. Then they assume that the candidate has demonstrated performance and will continue to do so in the new job.

Recently, we developed interviewing questions for a large manufacturing client. When describing the job barriers, the client identified a set of situations that new hires need to be able to perform but that recent hires could not. We asked the client, "How did you assess the ability of recent hires to handle these situations?" The client answered, "I didn't. The candidates we interviewed all worked for a very well-regarded organization, and I assumed that with their experiences they would automatically be able to handle our situations."

Assuming That Employees Will Be Successful Only Under Ideal Work Conditions

Interviewers like to ask questions such as "What would your ideal job be?" or "What were the favorite and least favorite parts of your previous job?" These questions are based on the assumption that comparing the candidate's preferences to the realities of the open position will yield important information about the candidate's ability to meet performance expectations. If the candidate doesn't describe an ideal job that matches the one under consideration, the interviewer assumes that the candidate will not enjoy the job, will therefore perform poorly, and will quit shortly after employment.

This assumption is easy to debunk. Think of a job that was not ideal but that you enjoyed and stayed at for a significant amount of time, and in which you were viewed as a good performer. Most people can cite several examples. If workers will stay, enjoy, and be good at jobs that are not ideal, we should not use this as the standard to assess the match between the applicant and the job.

For similar reasons, questions about least and most favorite parts of jobs should also be avoided as measures of the candidate's competency. Think of a job that you really liked and were good at. Was there a part of that job that you disliked? Alternatively, if someone says they liked something about their last job, does that mean that they won't like a new job because the same something won't be a part of it? Have you ever left a job that you liked, gone to a job that had nothing in common with your old job, and found that you liked the new job more? We know many people for whom this has been true. Questions about favorite past activities only focus on limited aspects of a job. More important, these questions do not measure an applicant's competencies for a specific job. They are not good questions for selecting employees.

Yet "ideal job" and "least and most favorite part" questions can be good questions for purposes other than hiring. They can be useful for placement of an employee in a particular job. Placement is a different process that involves assessing what is the optimal position to place a candidate who is qualified for a range of positions. Placement should occur after selection since it doesn't make any sense to place someone in a job for which they are not qualified. The point is not to use placement questions as the basis for selection.

Assuming That Candidates' Ability to Sell Themselves Predicts Their Ability to Do the Job

This assumption is reflected in questions such as "Why should I hire you?" and "What do you know about us?" The logic behind this assumption is that the positive, high-energy candidate will be interested in doing the job and will be a highly motivated employee. But are interviewers really measuring interest in doing the job—or interest in *getting* the job? Interviewers who focus on the applicant's energetic communication style often mistakenly infer the applicant will have the same positive, energetic approach on the job.

Another possibility is that the interviewer's own energetic style may be influencing the applicant's behaviors. Researchers have found that interviewees often model an interviewer's verbal and nonverbal communication behaviors.[7] As a result, the energetic interviewer finds the interaction with the energetic, positive candidate comfortable and assumes the candidate will be a good fit for the job.

While it is true that most managers want to hire positive, energetic employees, the problem with this assumption is that we are not measuring specific performance expectations related to the job. If you ask a manager why they want someone with a positive, energetic style, you're apt to hear that the new employee needs to be able to overcome tough customer service challenges. Or another expectation the manager might have is that the new employee, when faced with an unhappy customer, will focus on keeping a positive attitude while working to resolve the complaint. If these are the expectations that managers are interested in, the most accurate assessment will occur if they measure them directly.

Similarly, interviewers assume that a candidate who has researched the company and knows something about it is the candidate who will be well-prepared and interested on the job. What is really being measured is preparation for an interview, which may not necessarily predict the type of preparation the candidate needs to perform the job. Every professional interviewee knows how to show enthusiasm and research the company. These questions are often a better measurement of interviewing skills than of the ability to meet performance expectations.

Assuming That Asking Non-Job-Related Questions Will Reveal Relevant Job Behaviors

This faulty assumption leads interviewers to ask questions such as "If you were a vegetable, what kind would you be?" or "Tell me about your life in one or two sentences." With these questions, the interviewer is playing psychologist, trying to get a deep insight into the applicant's personality. To make an accurate assessment using non-job-related questions, the interviewer has to infer important job behaviors from the candidate's response. This is a long, dubious leap.

Exhibit 4.1 contains non-job-related questions that interviewers have shared with us. These questions convey a negative image about the organization to the candidate because of the irrelevance of the answers in predicting competency requirements. Would you be attracted to an organization that measured your competencies with these questions?

■ Valid Assumptions Behind Effective Interviewing Questions

Why do you ask the interview questions that you do? What are the assumptions behind your questions? Two valid assumptions are the basis for effective interview questions:

- Measurements of past behavior are good predictors of future behavior. They tend to reveal whether the candidate's competencies will match performance expectations.
- Questions that are closely linked to performance expectations are likely to reveal the candidate's ability to perform on the job.

Exhibit 4.1. Ineffective Questions Asked in Interviews

1. What is your favorite movie?
2. What is your favorite food?
3. How would you go about filling this room with balloons?
4. Describe the things you did this morning before you came to see us.
5. There is one play left in the football game. The defensive team is ahead by six points. The offensive team has the ball on the other team's one-yard line. Would you rather be on offense or defense and why?

Assuming That Past Behavior Can Indicate Future Performance

Measuring past behavior to predict future performance results in more precise measurement than inferences based on an attempt to measure attitudes, values, or beliefs. Interviewers who say they are interested in "someone with a good attitude" or "someone who shares the organization's values" probably believe that they can infer desirable job behaviors based on the candidate's responses. If interviewers are interested in job behaviors, measuring behaviors will lead directly to what they want to know.

Sometimes people claim that if you ask candidates direct questions about past behaviors, they can lie. However, candidates can lie about their attitudes and values as well as they lie about behaviors. As we will note in Chapter Five, probing the candidate's answers for specific behaviors can help you identify when lying may be a concern. For now, asking what you want to know is the obvious path to achieving the most precise measurement.

Assuming That Accurate Measurement of Job Performance Links Behaviors to Performance Expectations

Even if you measure a specific job behavior precisely, this doesn't mean that is the job behavior you should be measuring. The second assumption is that questions should be tightly linked to performance expectations and cover all three components: goals, job barriers, and competency requirements. These questions will allow you to more accurately predict the interviewee's ability to perform well on the job.

Many interviewers today focus on behavior, but they do not always know why they need to do it. Anyone can ask questions about behavior. Asking about the right behaviors and knowing how they connect to the job will enhance the ability of the interviewer to accurately measure the desired performance expectations.

Suppose an interviewer wants to measure whether a candidate can be an influential team member on a team that has stubbornly resisted change. The interviewer asks, "Give me an example of being a member of a team at work. What was your role?" This is a behaviorally based question, but it shows the interviewer isn't really sure why the question is being posed. An interviewer who is interested in the candidate's ability to be effective on a team that has resisted change needs to ask a question that links team behaviors to the specific job barriers that the candidate will need to overcome—resistance to change. An example of such a question is: "Give me an example of being a member of a team at work—a team that had members who were more focused on preserving the status quo than trying something new. Describe what you did in this situation and why you did it."

Try it yourself. Think about one or two of your best interview questions. Ask what the answer to your question tells you about the candidate's behavior. Then ask how that information helps you understand the potential for effectiveness on the job. The last part is the strategic link that interviewers often overlook.

■ Strategies for Effective Interview Questions

The following strategies are based on the valid assumptions behind effective interview questions.

Strategy 1: Ask for a Demonstration

It is particularly useful to ask candidates to demonstrate their behavior for the specific types of situations that are key to successful job performance. After all, one of the best ways to measure whether candidates can do something is to ask them to do it.[8] This is the idea behind performance or work sample requests that are often integrated into the interview process.[9] Done well, work samples are tightly linked to behaviors that define effective job performance. There is no gap between what is measured in the interview and the desired job behavior because the person performs the desired behavior during the interview.

A manager might think a good work sample for a sales job would be to pick up a pen and say, "Sell me this pen." But unless the sales applicant is applying for a job selling pens, this is not likely to be an effective work sample.

To be an effective work sample or performance question, what is measured in the interview should be similar to the job in terms of

- Time to perform the task
- Activities involved
- Work conditions
- Frequency
- Importance
- Performance standards

The "sell me this pen" request fails these criteria in many ways. For example, most salespeople have the opportunity to prepare presentations and become knowledgeable about their products. You are not hiring someone to sell something on the spur of the moment.

One way to create a work sample question would be to actually try and simulate the work environment as much as possible. This might involve informing the candidate prior to the interview that the process will involve giving a brief sales presentation on a familiar product. Instead of inferring performance, the interviewer can observe it. But the interviewer needs to observe performance in those key (job barrier) situations that determine success.

Strategy 2: Ask for Descriptions of Past Experience with Job Barriers

Obviously, it is not always practical or possible to observe performance. Instead, the interviewer can describe a specific situation the applicant would face on the job and listen for evidence that the applicant can demonstrate the expected behavior. To implement this strategy effectively, the interviewer needs to know the key job barriers to ask about and how the candidate should achieve goals and overcome job barriers.

Using this strategy, you would avoid a question such as "Give me an example of a time you dealt with a difficult customer. What did you do?" Since the question does not clearly define the situation, the candidate may not be able to describe expected job behaviors. Perhaps the candidate has dealt with many difficult customers. Which one would make the best example? To help the candidate provide the best example, the interviewer needs to know what the situation is supposed to reveal and describe it accurately. Thus the interviewer might ask, "Give me an example in which you dealt with a difficult customer who had a valid complaint against your organization." The greater the specificity of this second question, assuming it is a key to successful job performance, the more likely the candidate will select an appropriate example to describe.

Experts differ about whether the question should be worded to ask what candidates have done in the situation or what they would do. We recommend the following sequence:

1. Ask how the candidate has behaved in the specific situation.
2. If the candidate has not been in the situation, ask how the candidate has behaved in similar situations.
3. If the candidate has not been in similar situations, ask how the candidate would behave in the situation.

The logic of asking for specific examples of how someone has behaved is that it aids the probing process, which we will discuss in more detail in the next chapter. There is research evidence to support the idea that asking applicants how they have behaved can be a better predictor of future behavior than asking how they would behave.[10] Here we will just note that it is easier to probe when someone describes what they have done than when they describe what they say they will do.

Strategy 3: Ask for Descriptions of Behavior in Comparable Situations

Most interviewers recognize the value of asking candidates to demonstrate or describe past behaviors that are closely linked to the desired job behaviors. However, they may wonder whether this approach is only useful for experienced individuals since it is asking about specific job-related situations. Strategy 3 acknowledges that individuals may have faced many situations that are similar in terms of the competency requirements needed to handle them effectively, even though they took place in different contexts. For example, in almost every job, one of the keys to success is the ability to deal with too much work in too short a time.

Applying Strategy 3, an effective interviewer might ask "Can you give me an example in which your boss asked you to do "x, y, and z," all equally important, and they could not be done at the same time? What did you do?" Inexperienced candidates may respond that they have never had that happen on any job in which they worked because they never did "x, y, or z" on a job.

Yet an inexperienced candidate may have demonstrated great competency in balancing other "x, y, and z" elements at school, or in personal life. The problem is that many inexperienced candidates do not recognize the similarity of the situations and so fail to describe their competencies. Interviewers who ask effective questions know that the specific behaviors of interest for determining job success are not just finishing tasks "x, y, and z" but knowing how to handle situations when there are competing and equally important priorities. Interviewers also recognize that this competency requirement can be developed outside the job. Thus the more effective interviewer might ask, "Can you give me an example in which you had several things that needed to be done at the same time and were of equal importance? What did you do? You can use work or nonwork experiences to describe the situation." For this strategy to be successful, the interviewer must know how a well-qualified candidate would behave and recognize that the competency requirement can be demonstrated in a range of similar situations.

Strategy 4: Ask How Past Behavior Relates to the Performance Expectations

The strategies we have discussed so far link what the question measures to what the job requires. Strategy 4 also asks candidates to consider how past behaviors demonstrate they can meet performance expectations. To use this strategy, the interviewer can ask, "Could you give me some examples of how your work experiences qualify you for this position?" Because this question is linked to the specific job, it is more effective than the often-used introductory question "Tell me about yourself," to which many candidates do not know how to respond.

This approach provides several benefits. First, it allows you to guide the candidate to provide a more focused answer; it explains the objective of the question without specifying the answer. A second benefit is that the interviewer acquires some context to understand the interviewee's past behaviors and assess the connection to the desired job situations. Third, candidates who may not have had the required job experience can demonstrate how comparable experience allowed them to develop the competency requirements needed to meet desired performance expectations.

For example, one of the job barriers for an effective sales-person might be encountering rejection. The effective salesperson might be one who has to uncover the reason for a rejection and go back with a new strategy to meet the person's needs. Trainers may go through a similar process with difficult trainees. The effective trainer who demonstrates resiliency by winning over difficult trainees after many failed attempts may have demonstrated one of the key competency requirements for a sales job without ever encountering the rejection of a sales call.

Similarly, a CEO of an organization recently told us that his music education was very beneficial to his business since the composing aspect required him to look at all the different parts and make sure they were in sync—and this is what he did in business. Asking "What is your educational background?" would not uncover this competency. Asking "How has your education prepared you for this job?" or "How would you apply your education to this job?" increases the likelihood that interviewees will be able to connect their past behaviors to the job.

This strategy can enhance the applicant pool by identifying people who may not typically have been considered for a position. However, this may reduce the accuracy of assessing competency requirements since it relies on both the candidate's and interviewer's judgment to connect these divergent experiences to those required on the job. And once the connection is made, you still must make sure that you are gathering information related to the specific desired behaviors.

Strategy 5: Ask for Descriptions of Accomplishments

Ask candidates to describe how they meet competency requirements or produce accomplishments for their organization. As noted earlier, performance expectations have three aspects—goals, job barriers, and competency requirements. Strategies 1 through 4 focus more on job barriers and competency requirements; Strategy 5 focuses more on accomplishments. For example, Strategy 5 suggests asking, "Give me an example of a time when your attention to detail has benefited your organization." Or you could ask, "What have you done to make your organization more effective?"

These questions also open up the pool of applicants by recognizing individuals who have the desired accomplishments or similar ones. Interviewers hire people because they want them to make their organizations better. People who have made things better in the past are more likely to make things better in the future. However, interviewers can make the mistake of hiring people who produce a good outcome by using a bad process. Likewise, interviewers must be attentive to the opposite concern of people who use the right process but never seem to produce the desired outcomes. These questions are designed to address what was accomplished and how it was accomplished.

In Figure 4.1, the concentric rings illustrate the connection between performance expectations and the effectiveness of the questioning strategy. The closer the link is between the question and desired performance expectations, the more effective the questioning strategy. The connection is strongest between performance expectations (the center of the circle) and the first ring, questions that ask a candidate to demonstrate the behavior expected on the job. As the interview moves to the second and third rings, from describing past behavior in the specific situation to describing past behavior in comparable situations, the connection between the question and performance expectations progressively decreases. The next ring asks the candidate to connect past behavior to performance expectations. The candidate's behavior may have occurred in situations different from those expected on the job but demonstrating the same competency requirements. The outermost ring asks how a candidate meets competency requirements and produces accomplish-

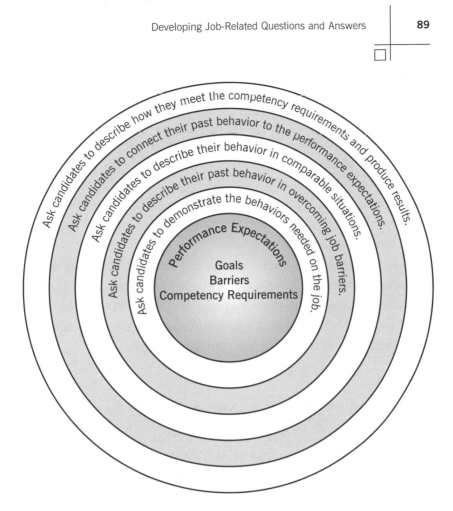

Figure 4.1. Connection Between Performance Expectations and Questioning Strategy

ments. This ring is the farthest from the center because the interviewer must link the competency requirements and accomplishments to the performance expectations of the job.

Appendix A at the end of the book explains how we would rate the questions in Assessment 4.1 and our rationale for our ratings. Before you look at the appendix, go back to the Assessment and take a minute to rethink your initial ratings to see how you would rate these questions now. Make sure you also have a reason for why you rated the question either effective or ineffective.

■ Identifying Answers That Demonstrate the Candidate's Ability to Meet Performance Expectations

Most interviewers spend considerably more time on creating or choosing questions than on determining answers to the questions. Some interviewers say that they don't have answers in mind because they are asking questions "to get a feel for how the candidate thinks." Other interviewers say they will know the right answer when they hear it.

In this section, we will discuss the mistake of letting applicant answers set the standards for the selection decision and the wisdom of measuring candidate answers against an objective standard. We will also provide some strategies for developing answers that can serve as objective standards.

Why Applicant Answers Must Not Set the Standards

If interviewers don't take the time to think about the answers they are looking for, they are most likely using candidates as the source of effective answers. Unfortunately, this often happens. Interviewers compare the answers of various candidates to determine who should be hired. After conducting several interviews, the interviewer sits back and thinks, "I wasn't impressed with Nick's answer to the questions on problem solving," or "Lauren seemed to know more about teams than she did about other things. Kate didn't fall flat on any of the questions and she had the best style, so I think I'm going to hire her."

The flaw in this approach is that Kate may be an unqualified worker who appears to be qualified because the other candidates are even more unqualified. Not having taken the time to know what to look for, the interviewer turns to the candidates and lets the best answer, whether effective or ineffective, become the standard.

Why Objective Standards Are Important

Although it is necessary to compare candidates to make a hiring decision, the best way to do so is to compare each candidate to an objective standard or answer determined by the interviewer prior to asking the questions. Comparing candidates to a pre-determined standard results in two key benefits.

First, the standard helps interviewers focus their probing to determine if the candidate can meet the competency requirements. Without answers, interviewers don't know what they are trying to find out when they probe for more information. If they don't know what they are looking for, how will they know it when they see it? As noted in Chapter One, finding well-qualified candidates in a tight labor market can be very difficult. Therefore, it is even more important than ever before not to give in and simply hire the best of a limited pool.

Second, interviewers can use the information they gather to identify areas for development to help candidates who are acceptable but not best qualified. This can create early management successes with new employees. Managers can have a positive impact on the early success of new hires because they have a clear definition of performance standards. For example, new employees can be better matched to initial job assignments based on a better assessment of their skills.

This can also lead to early coaching and initial training that addresses performance problems before they occur. The result should be more positive performance appraisals because the performance gaps are identified and resolved early in the job. Most important, the information gathered can become a recruiting enticement. An initial job offer can be accompanied by an assessment of the candidate and plans to develop skills to cover specific performance gaps. Letting candidates know that you care about their development and have a plan to address skill gaps can lead good people to prefer your job offer over other opportunities. Highly qualified candidates are usually motivated to further enhance their skills. An offer to both hire and develop the employee can be an effective recruitment and retention strategy.

Strategies for Developing Answers to Interviewing Questions

- *Strategy 1: Develop samples of both effective and ineffective answers.*

  Remember that answers are designed to differentiate among levels of a performance expectation, so you need to identify both effective and ineffective answers. The sample effective answer may be very similar to the definition of the competency requirement. However, the ineffective answer is needed to help identify when a candidate falls below an acceptable level of the performance expectation.

- *Strategy 2: View the answers you prepare as samples that reflect a range of effective and ineffective answers.*

  For example, "attempted to get to the true source of the client's problem" is a sample effective answer that might apply to a variety of specific responses. The interviewer will listen to the applicant's answer and determine if it is similar to the examples of behaviors that would demonstrate meeting the competency requirements for the job.

- *Strategy 3: Prepare answers that are as behaviorally specific as possible and focus on actions.*

  As with competency requirement definitions, what distinguishes an effective from an ineffective answer should be easily recognizable by others.

Appendix B at the end of the book provides an example of job barriers, competency requirements, interview questions, and effective and ineffective answers for a sales position.

■ Avoiding Discrimination Complaints with Effective Questions and Answers

You may be wondering why we have not yet addressed the issue of discrimination in the interview process. Untrained interviewers are often very interested in knowing what they can and cannot ask. Exhibit 4.2 gives advice about avoiding a number of specific issues it's illegal to raise with applicants.

Rather than focusing on what questions to avoid, it is much better to focus on knowing what you really need to ask in the interview process so as to measure the applicant's ability to do the job. Interviewers who focus on measuring an applicant's ability to do the job correctly minimize their vulnerability to losing discrimination lawsuits as a result of the nature of the interview

---

Exhibit 4.2. A Sample of Interview Topics Forbidden by Law

- Don't ask if an applicant is single, married, divorced, or separated, unless this information is job-related (and it is very unlikely to be).
- Don't ask the ages of an applicant's children. This question might lead to charges of sex discrimination if you decide not to hire a woman who has small children at home.
- Don't ask about pregnancy or plans for a family. An interviewer may ask how long the applicant plans to stay on the job and whether any absences are anticipated—if the same questions are asked of males and females.
- Don't ask someone's age or date of birth. This might lead to age discrimination. You may ask if the applicant is between the ages of eighteen and seventy, and if the answer is no, it is permissible to inquire about the exact age.
- Don't ask if the applicant has ever been arrested. You may ask if the applicant has been convicted of a felony, but only if this is clearly job-related.
- Don't ask about a person's birthplace, ancestry, or "native tongue." The answers might indicate national origin.
- Don't ask for a maiden name or the name of the next of kin. Again the matter of national origin is involved. But it is legal to ask for the names of relatives who already work for your organization or for competing firms.

questions that are asked. Interviewers who use the approach we recommend would not ask questions about personal characteristics, they would instead focus on job-related behaviors.

Even if interviewers do not focus on personal characteristics, discrimination can occur. *Adverse impact* is a type of employment discrimination that occurs when a particular selection device, such as an interview, disproportionately rejects one group of applicants (minorities, women, or whatever). Job-relatedness is the best defense against discrimination accusations based on adverse impact. Doing the right thing—gathering job-related information to predict performance expectations—protects your organization against losing to charges alleging this type of discrimination.[11] In the next chapter, we will discuss discrimination in terms of organizing and conducting the interview.

CHAPTER SUMMARY

In this chapter, we discussed the assumptions that lie behind ineffective and effective interview questions. We presented specific strategies for developing job-related questions and answers prior to conducting the interview. The closer the link between the performance expectation and the question, the more effective the questioning strategy. Asking the candidate to perform the desired behavior in the interview is the most effective strategy, followed by asking the candidate to describe past behaviors in similar situations. Asking the candidate to describe behaviors in situations different from the job is less effective because the link to the performance expectation is weaker. Finally, asking candidates to describe past accomplishments may reveal competencies, but the connection to the open position depends on the interviewer's assessment of the link to required performance expectations.

Preparing the list of questions and sample effective and ineffective answers ahead of time keeps the interviewer focused and can have a positive impact on the initial success of new hires through definition of objective standards and more precise measurement. This can be a powerful recruiting tool because it tells candidates both that your organization will measure what they can do and that it will also help them identify ways to improve their performance.

Chapter Five will provide more strategies regarding the use of questions, such as how to sequence them in the interview to elicit the best candidate input and how to use follow-up questions to probe for specific information.

Finally, in the following "Perspectives" three managers who have used the Strategic Interviewing Approach describe how the interviewing questions they use today differ from questions they have used in the past.

Perspectives on Interview Questions

Susan Mason, Vice President of Human Resources,
Old Kent Financial Services

How are the types of questions different from the ones that were previously asked? Is there a difference in how you probe or determine the correct answers to interview questions?

Our interviewers ask focused questions based on the competencies required. Using focused questions together with effective probing techniques, we are able to obtain specific, detailed information from the candidate. We have also found that candidates are more at ease describing fact-based experiences, rather than focusing on whether they have answered the question "correctly." For example, "Tell me about a time you managed your staff through a change or a crisis situation" is more effective than "Tell me where you want to be in five years." The questions we ask today tend to be more job-related, more behaviorally focused, and more probing in nature.

Our interviewer styles are also more consistent as this questioning process focuses on the candidate with the interviewer taking the role of the active listener.

Mike Johnson, Human Resources Manager, Plante & Moran

How are the types of questions different from the ones that were previously asked? Is there a difference in how you probe or determine the correct answers to interview questions?

Our questions are dramatically different. The type of questions we ask now are open-ended, yet strategic. They are not "tell me about yourself" type questions. They are open-ended enough that their answers can trigger an opportunity to probe, yet they are not so vague that they lack strategy.

In terms of answers, what started this process for us was our strategic plan. We created a performance management system to gather the troops and focus our resources on achieving the plan. The competency requirements we need to achieve our strategic goals are in that plan. Basically the correct answers to the interview questions are driven by our performance management system and what we need to find in people and develop in people in order to succeed as a firm.

In my view, the correct answers are critical for the interviewer to do a good job of probing. It is really difficult to question someone if you don't know why you are asking the question and you don't know what the right answer is. I think the quality of probing increases dramatically if you understand why you are asking this more direct and focused question. If you just gave the interviewer the right questions and answers, that would not be enough because your ability to probe is the freestyle portion of the interview that allows you to make sure that you are getting to the true objective of the questions. And if you don't truly understand why the question is being asked, you will never be able to do that.

Susan J. Adams, Chief of Recruitment, International Monetary Fund

How are the types of questions different from the ones that were previously asked? Is there a difference in how you probe or determine the correct answers to interview questions?

The questions we now ask in interviews are much better articulated than in the past, in part because we have agreed in advance to the type of answer we are listening for. We ask the question very clearly to draw out specific information (but still without giving away *too* much!). There is much less "hemming and hawing" among the panelists in our team interviews as they pose questions; they look like they have their act together more!

The interviewers I have observed are now very directed in their follow-up probes, specifically because they are trying to score candidates' answers against agreed acceptable/unacceptable standards. Candidates are pleasantly surprised by this difference in probing, and some have noted after the interview that they were happy to see how closely the interviewers listened to their answers in the follow-up questions.

In the past, we had no standard to determine correct answers to interview questions; it was left up to the judgment of the interviewers. Now we have pre-agreed standards and preferred language and approach for specific questions, with parameters for success rather than *exact* straitjacket expectations. This has made our assessments much more accurate, even using these ranges of guidelines rather than expected exact scripts.

Applications

1. What are the assumptions behind the questions you currently ask in your interviews?
2. What past behaviors do you use to predict future job behaviors?
3. How do you link questions to desired job performance?
4. What questions in your interviews are likely to lead to truthful answers? What questions merely measure opinions?
5. How are you making sure your questions measure success rather than experience?

Conducting an Effective Interview

How you conduct your interviews plays an important role in your ability to accurately measure whether interviewees can meet your performance expectations. In the preceding chapters, we have described the steps to prepare effectively for an interview: (1) Set goals and manage the process. (2) Identify the performance expectations that differentiate levels of job performance. (3) Develop questions to measure the behaviors that demonstrate the candidate can meet or exceed performance expectations. (4) Determine the types of responses that indicate the correct and incorrect answers so you can accurately assess whether the candidate's competencies are a good match for the job.

You can follow all of the steps up to this point and still fail to hire a talented employee if you conduct your interview poorly. A number of circumstances can detract from your ability to accurately measure the candidate:

- Misunderstanding the true meaning of a question may cause a candidate to give an answer that appears to be incorrect.
- Misinterpreting the true meaning of an answer may cause an interviewer to rate a qualified candidate as not meeting performance expectations.
- Anxiety may reduce the candidate's ability to fully comment on ways to meet performance expectations.
- Distractions such as phone calls or other interruptions may cause the interviewer or interviewee to lose their concentration or interest.
- Fatigue on the part of the interviewer or interviewee may also cause a loss of concentration or an inaccurate picture of the candidate's true abilities.

Almost everyone who has conducted an interview or been interviewed has experienced some of these circumstances. When these events occur, interviewers tend to rely on their impressions or "gut-level reactions"—and as a result, their chances of conducting a successful interview decline.[1] If a good selection decision occurs, it happens more by chance than by the interviewer's skill.

Conducting a strategic interview may also require more discipline because you will need to have a strategy to minimize circumstances that prevent accurate measurement. In this chapter, we will discuss the typical problems that occur in conducting interviews and the strategies to prevent problems so that you can accurately assess whether the candidate has the competencies to succeed in the job.

Before we move to this discussion, complete Assessment 5.1. Evaluate the frequency that you use the named strategies to conduct interviews.

> **■ Assessment 5.1. ■**
> **Strategies for Conducting an Effective Interview**
>
> 1. Before conducting an interview, I develop an interviewer guide that identifies job barriers and competency requirements and corresponding questions and answers.
>
>   ☐ Always   ☐ Most of the time   ☐ Sometimes   ☐ Never
>
> 2. When conducting an interview, I follow an interviewer guide, asking all the candidates all of the questions.
>
>   ☐ Always   ☐ Most of the time   ☐ Sometimes   ☐ Never
>
> 3. When conducting an interview, I take detailed notes to recall the candidate's past behaviors after the interview.
>
>   ☐ Always   ☐ Most of the time   ☐ Sometimes   ☐ Never
>
> 4. When conducting an interview, I probe the candidate's responses to understand how the candidate has behaved, not to obtain the right answer.
>
>   ☐ Always   ☐ Most of the time   ☐ Sometimes   ☐ Never
>
> 5. When conducting an interview, I remove all distractions, both auditory and visual, so that each party can easily communicate with the other.
>
>   ☐ Always   ☐ Most of the time   ☐ Sometimes   ☐ Never
>
> 6. To reduce duplication and exhaustion of multiple back-to-back interviews, my organization uses team interviews.
>
>   ☐ Always   ☐ Most of the time   ☐ Sometimes   ☐ Never
>
> As you read this chapter, you will learn why each of these strategies will help you to conduct more effective interviews.

■ Problems That Lead to Poorly Conducted Interviews

Even when interviewers have carefully prepared for interviews, they can have problems that will result in poorly conducted interviews. Typical problems include unstructured or poorly structured interviews, environmental distractions, and multiple back-to-back interviews.

Poorly Structured Interviews

Some interviewers will use the interview time to verify information on the résumé or application. We call this the "tell me a little bit" interview. For example, the interviewer might begin by saying, "I see that your last position was with Company X. Tell me a little bit about that job." This continues as the interviewer moves through the resume, each time saying, "Tell me a little bit about that." As the candidate responds to the requests for details about résumé entries, the interviewer may or may not interrupt to probe the candidate's responses. Actually, the interviewer is letting the candidate's résumé drive the interview, instead of focusing on performance expectations. While the interviewer does gather information, it is dictated in large part by the candidate's résumé strategies rather than by the interviewer's information-gathering strategies.

Not surprisingly, some candidates prefer interviews that focus on the résumé because they believe they have more control over the process. Interviewers who rely on résumés relinquish control because their strategy for gathering information is to let candidates do the talking and hope they will say something that demonstrates that they are qualified for the job. This approach is like looking for a needle in a haystack. You are looking for a good employee. But since you are not sure what information will demonstrate that the candidate will meet your expectations, you end up gathering different types of information from various candidates in your search for that good employee.

Interviewers who do not follow a structured, job-driven process may also spend much of their time engaged in small talk, characterized by brief discussions on a variety of topics such as the weather, the interviewee's travel to the company, or perceptions of the company or the local area. While conversations between strangers are often dominated by these generic topics, too much small talk in an interview takes valuable time away from assessment.

Small talk may mislead candidates about the quality of their performance in the interview. A candidate may think the easy conversation indicates the interviewer is favorably impressed and plans to offer a job. Interviewers who rely on small talk make judgments based on whether they connect with the candidate— they have nothing else to use in making their assessment. Although interviewers are not expected to hire people they dislike, liking someone is not a good reason for offering employment.

Interviewers who have not structured their process are also likely to ask different questions of different candidates. As a result, the interviewers will not necessarily use the same standards to assess all applicants for the same position.[2] They may conduct a free-form interview, asking questions with no particular order or logic. When interviewers expect applicants to continually switch their perspectives as they jump from topic to topic, the effect can be to heighten the applicants' anxiety and cause more measurement problems.

Environmental Distractions

Both interviewers and candidates can be hindered by a poor interviewing environment. Some environments block effective listening and communication. The interviewing room, its size, lighting, comfort level, seating arrangements, and the presence of external distractions such as ringing phones, computer screens, and outside windows can take both participants' attention away from their interaction. These distractions make it harder for candidates to communicate their competencies and harder for the interviewer to focus on gathering key information for a hiring decision.

A nervous but competent candidate can be easily distracted and can end up sounding incompetent. Even confident candidates can be distracted in a poor environment. Candidates often describe how a huge desk created a physical barrier that seemed to inhibit communication or how interruptions broke the flow of an interview. One interviewee described an extremely distracting environment as "a table in a restaurant next to a big-screen TV tuned in to a soap opera. A woman on the program was giving birth. The interviewer conducted the entire interview during this birthing scene, which seemed to go on forever."

Even more than distracting, some environments can be very uncomfortable for a candidate. Women interviewees have described being interviewed in a hotel guest room by a male interviewer. "He sat on one bed, and I sat on the other. I was very uncomfortable." Clearly, this type of environment is not merely uncomfortable—it also creates an unprofessional impression of the interviewer and of the hiring organization.

Multiple Back-to-Back Interviews

In many organizations, a number of interviewers need to interview the candidate, who typically endures multiple one-on-one interviews, one right after the other. As we noted in Chapter Two, interviewers may be asking the same questions and creating the impression that the organization is not very organized. More important, the sequence also creates an impression that the interviewers have little respect for the candidate's time. Many candidates report going through as many as six or seven hour-long interviews in one day. If you have had that experience, you know that you feel mentally and emotionally exhausted at the end of the day. The hiring organization seems to be saying, "We want to welcome you into our organization, if you let us beat you up first." Clearly, this is a turnoff to high-quality talent.

Multiple back-to-back interviews can create interviewee anxiety since a candidate may have difficulty keeping all the names straight and remembering what was said in which interview. Multiple back-to-back interviews can also lead to inaccurate measurement since fatigue may cause the candidate to process a question inaccurately or even to forget a correct answer.

Interviewers such as college recruiters who interview multiple candidates in back-to-back interviewers also experience fatigue that can reduce their ability to listen carefully and process candidates' responses. College recruiters admit that they typically are not as good at evaluating candidates in their eighth or ninth interview of the day as they were in their first or second interview.

■ Strategies for Conducting Effective Interviews

Effective interviews don't just happen. They occur because interviewers use strategies to avoid the problems we have discussed. The most effective strategies include developing and using an interviewer guide, previewing the interview process for the candidate, probing to gather more complete behavioral data, reinforcing the impressions you want to create, managing the interviewing environment, and streamlining the interview process with team interviews.

Strategy 1: Develop and Use an Interviewer Guide

Developing and using an interviewer guide ensures that interviewers ask all candidates for the same job a common set of questions and that the questions are organized in a way to strengthen accuracy of measurement.[3] An interviewer guide is essentially a plan for conducting your interview. The guide contains the materials you developed identifying performance expectations and formulating questions and answers as outlined in earlier chapters. As discussed in Chapter Two, you also need to minimize redundancies among interviewers so that the candidates are not answering the same questions in every interview. Exhibit 5.1 lists some recommendations for developing an interviewer guide.

You should develop interviewer guides for all interviews that are designed to measure candidates, including both team and individual interviews. At first glance, formulating guides may seem to be a lot of work. But consider these four advantages:

- Only the measurement section of the guide is likely to change much from one guide to the next. Although there should be different interviewer guides for different jobs, most guides will probably be quite similar except for the questions and sample responses and the logic behind them.
- You will save time when preparing for subsequent interviews and subsequent rounds of hiring for the same job. To conduct an effective interview, you need to prepare and integrate all of the material that exists in the guide. To do this each time a job becomes available would be a time-consuming task. Assuming that the core performance expectations remain relatively stable, an interviewer guide will substantially cut the time it takes to prepare for subsequent interviews.
- Using a well-developed interviewer guide reduces an organization's vulnerability to employment discrimination

Exhibit 5.1. Guidelines for Developing an Interviewer Guide

- *Begin with general guidelines for interviewers to follow in conducting their interviews.*

  Your guidelines should instruct interviewers to ask all questions of all candidates so that candidates will not be treated differently during the interviewing process. Add other reminders about avoiding topics that might create discrimination complaints, such as questions on age, race, or marital status. Also, suggest that the interviewers take notes describing the candidate's responses.

- *Tell the interviewer how to start the interview.*

  Suggest that the interviewer begin the interview by providing information to the candidate about the interview process. If the candidate has several interviews scheduled, discuss who the candidate will be meeting and the general focus of each interview. For example, you might say that the human resources professional will ask questions and talk about company benefits while the department manager will ask questions to verify that the candidate understands the major duties and responsibilities of the job. In describing the general focus of the interviews, avoid details that reveal to candidates the standards that interviewers will use to assess their answers.

- *Create a measurement section in the interviewer guide.*

  In this measurement section, list the performance expectation, the question or questions that measure it, and sample effective and ineffective answers. Often guides include only the questions or the questions and sample answers. Including each goal that needs to be achieved, what needs to get done (overcoming the job barrier) to achieve that goal, and how someone needs to behave to get it done (the competency requirement) keeps the interviewer focused on why he or she is asking a question. Having all this information allows interviewers to make judgments about whether the candidate can meet the job's performance expectations.

- *Organize the questions so that there is a logical flow to the interview.*

  Group questions together that address similar topics. Organize the material by beginning with questions that the candidate should be able to answer easily to build the candidate's confidence. Proceed toward more challenging

Exhibit 5.1. Guidelines for Developing an Interviewer Guide (cont.)

questions, and postpone questions that focus on how the candidate's accomplishments demonstrate an ability to do the job until near the end of the interview. These are typically more difficult questions because they ask the candidate to connect past accomplishments to the job's requirements.

- *Include suggestions for closing the interview.*

  Remind the interviewer to make sure that the candidate's questions have been answered. Include suggestions for informing the candidate of the next steps in the process. Finally, provide recommended language for terminating the interview process.

complaints resulting from interviews.[4] Some discrimination complaints occur because applicants feel they are treated differently from others.[5] The use of a guide shows that you treat all applicants the same and assess them against the same standards.

- Most important, using an interviewer guide requires managers to put their performance expectations on paper. The process of writing out these standards can make managers aware of inconsistencies and ambiguities they need to examine. Dealing with these issues will make managers more successful not only in selection but in other performance management tasks such as delegation, training, coaching, counseling, and assessing performance because the standards will be clear and consistent.

Better managers attract and are more likely to retain better employees. Managers know the importance of writing out their employees' performance appraisals. If this is important, isn't it worth the time to develop and define the standards that will become the basis for the appraisal?

Strategy 2: Preview the Interview Process for the Candidate

Gathering information from the candidate is the main focus of the interviewer during the interview. This section presents several recommendations for previewing the interview process so that the candidate knows what to expect and can communicate effectively with the interviewer.

- *Inform the candidate at the beginning of the interview why you are taking notes.*

Candidates often view note taking by the interviewer as a sign of right answers. You can unintentionally steer candidates to respond in ways they think might please you. You can inform the candidate that note taking is not a sign of a right or wrong answer but is used to help you remember key points. Taking detailed notes will help you to stay focused on understanding the candidate's behavior.[6] Unless you keep notes of the candidate's responses, some important behaviors may be forgotten.

- *Tell the candidate at the beginning of the interview that you will be probing their answers for additional information.*

Probing is one of the most important parts of the interview process. It means asking follow-up questions to gather more information or details. We will expand on strategies for behavioral probing later under Strategy 3.

Tell candidates that you will be doing this to better understand their responses. Tell them that if you interrupt them when they are answering a question, it won't mean that their answer is wrong, but rather that you are simply trying to understand more fully. Your explanation will usually help candidates view probing as a way to improve their answers.

We have polled numerous candidates on how they feel when an interviewer probes their answers for additional information. Most say they prefer probes as soon as they get off track as long as the interviewer does not appear to be interrogating them. However, cultural and individual differences can influence interviewees' reactions to probing, so it is important to explain what you are doing.

When is the right moment to probe? That will usually depend on the length of the interviewee's responses. One option is to wait until the candidate has completed an answer and then probe for more specifics. Another option is to probe by politely interrupting when the answer is not going in the right direction or lacks sufficient detail. Sometimes interviewers avoid interrupting because they feel it is rude. Professionally done, probing is a focused way to gather specific information. Failing to probe is unfair to the candidate since it allows someone to go in the wrong direction or give an incomplete answer. Even waiting to probe until the end of the candidate's response can be an ineffective use of the interview time.

- *Acknowledge that you have reviewed the résumé before you begin the interview.*

Using the Strategic Interviewing Approach, an interviewer does not need to review a résumé during the interview. With this approach, the job, not the résumé, drives the development of the questions and desired responses and should be the same across candidates for the same position. Résumés are not irrelevant, however, since they are usually used as an initial screening device to determine if the candidate meets the basic job requirements—a college education, for example.

Many candidates come to the interview prepared to discuss their résumés. Some may become concerned when interviewers do not ask questions about their résumés. They assume from this that the interviewer is unprepared or uninterested in them.

There are at least two strategies for dealing with this issue. The simplest is to inform the candidate as part of the introduction that you have reviewed the résumé, but that the interview will be a behavioral interview focused on the job requirements. You can also inform candidates that they can answer the question by highlighting data from their résumé or any aspect of their background that would apply.

A second strategy is to individualize the prepared questions with the candidate's résumé. If you do this, be sure to avoid making unwarranted assumptions or narrowing the candidate's possible response. For example, an interviewer might say, "Give me an example from your job at Company X when you led a team that had a team member who really did not pull his or her weight." In asking the question in this manner, the interviewer would be assuming that the candidate had a particular experience in a specific job and forcing the candidate to pick an example from that one experience, rather than to select from the total range of experiences. A better version of the question would be, "I noticed on your résumé that you worked at Company X and you led a team of marketing support staff. When you led that team, or any other team in your work experiences, was there ever a person on the team who really did not pull his or her weight? If this occurred, what did you do in this situation?"

- *Limit small talk at the beginning of the interview.*

Helping the candidate to feel relaxed and comfortable with some small talk will allow you to establish the rapport necessary for an effective interview.[7] At the same time, as we discussed earlier, too much small talk limits the time you will have to assess performance expectations. We suggest a "Warm—Focused—Warm" approach. Begin with a warm and friendly introduction—including a limited amount of small talk. Move from there to a focused and professional demeanor during the measurement portion of the interview. While you do not have to appear unfriendly, you do need to focus on assessing performance expectations. You are gathering information, not having a conversation, so you will make few personal comments during the measurement phase of the interview. At the end, while you are closing the interview, return to the warm and friendly style to leave a positive impression.

Strategy 3: Probe to Gather More Complete Behavioral Data

Candidates, even sophisticated ones, may respond to well-constructed behavioral questions with their opinions of what they did rather than accurate descriptions of the actions they took. For example, they say,

- I *led* the team.
- I *controlled* the budget.
- I applied my technical skills to *solve* the problem.

In each case, the italicized word reflects an ambiguous label. How did the person "lead" the team? There are many possibilities. One objective of behavioral probing is to uncover the true meaning of the actions behind the labels. When you hear words that could have multiple meanings, probe with questions such as these:

- What did you do?
- How did you do it?
- Why did you do it?

Often in response to probing questions, candidates still respond with labels. Part of the reason for this is that, like all of us, they often use labels in everyday language as shortcuts to communication.[8] As the interviewer, be assertive without being aggressive. Sometimes you will need to probe the same response more than once. Remember that the primary objective of probing is to understand how the candidate has behaved, not to obtain the right answer. Suspend your judgment during the interview.

You will know that sufficient probing has occurred when you can describe how the candidate has behaved. See whether you feel you could replicate the candidate's behavior, based on the response. For example, if someone said, "I resolved team conflict," would you be able to describe how that individual did so? Or if the candidate said, "I identified their common objectives and proposed sharing resources and restructuring the schedule," would you know how to replicate the behavior? Again, do not judge whether what the candidate did was the right thing to do, just make sure that you know exactly what actions the candidate took.

A second purpose of probing is to understand the outcomes of the candidate's actions. Even when candidates describe their actions, they often do not describe what resulted from the actions. Organizations are typically looking for individuals whose actions produced positive results. To understand what the candidate accomplished, you can ask one or more of these questions:

- What resulted from your actions?
- How did the organization benefit from your actions?
- Would you do anything differently and why?

This last probe is especially important and useful. The purpose of interviewing is to predict performance. This probe provides an indicator of how the candidate will behave, which is what we are trying to predict. Here are some more tactics for probing responses:

- *Ask how a candidate's behavior changed as a result of the experience.*

People often feel they learned something, when they really have not. For example, you could ask a candidate, "Did you learn anything from that action?" As the question is worded, this question measures opinion, rather than behavior. The key word should be *how*. A more effective probe would be, "How have you acted differently as a result of what you learned in this situation?" The idea is that if people learn something, they demonstrate it through their behavior.

- *Ask candidates about results.*

Some interviewers ask, "Did it work?" or "How did it work out?" These probes are not likely to lead to a truthful answer. Few candidates will admit, "It was a total failure." A better probe might be, "What resulted from what you did and how do you know this occurred?" or "How did you measure your success?"

- *Vary your style of probing to reduce a feeling of interrogation.*

If you continually use the same question format for your probes, your approach will eventually wear on candidates and make them feel that it is more an interrogation than an interview. One way to avoid this is to simply express an interest in more information, while at the same time demonstrating an appreciation of the challenges in the situation. (For example, you could say, "That must have been hard to do. How did you go about getting their approval?")

While we have suggested earlier the need to probe more than once to get a good understanding of how the candidate has behaved, sometimes "there is no there, there" and the candidate simply does not have a behavior to support a statement. Be alert to the need to back off when the candidate is unable to provide specifics.

- *Probe "red flags" but do not assume they are necessarily a bad sign.*

Red flags are comments that a candidate makes that leave the interviewer with the impression the candidate may have behaved inappropriately in a past situation. Often what the candidate reveals may initially seem to be a behavioral problem, but can actually be an indicator of a competency requirement. When probed, red flags reveal specific and important aspects of the candidate's behavior. In one interview, a candidate for executive director of a large not-for-profit agency revealed that she had left her last position because of a conflict with the board of directors. Naturally, this was a red flag for the board members who were conducting the interview, so they probed by asking her about the conflict and what she had done. In answering the question, the candidate explained that her former board had directed her to withhold certain financial information from a funding agency. While the directive might not have been illegal, she felt it was clearly unethical and resigned when she could not persuade the board to accept her recommendation. Only by probing for details could the interviewers get a clear understanding of the incident that led to the conflict and the candidate's behaviors in it.

- *Avoid the normal tendency to rush to judgment—take descriptive rather than evaluative notes and suspend judgment during the interview process.*

As an interviewer, you are like a reporter or journalist gathering the facts and putting them together to make the story. A good journalist would not write the story until all the facts were gathered. Unfortunately, some interviewers attempt to "write the story" by rushing to an opinion of a candidate before the facts are in. One way to control for this tendency is to take descriptive notes during the interview process. Focus your notes on describing the specific actions taken by the candidate, and avoid evaluative language and generic labels such as "did a good job" or "led the team."

In conjunction with the emphasis on description, focus the interview process on attaining the best understanding possible of what the candidate has done in situations similar to those that will determine success on the job. During the interview, the goal is not to judge whether the actions taken were the right ones. Interviewers who are making judgments when they should be gathering data are likely to miss important pieces of information and may fall into one of many judgment errors that we discuss in Chapter Six. Suspending judgment is a skill that requires discipline—most of us tend to rush to judgment when we first meet people and to form opinions based on our first impressions.

Strategy 4: Reinforce the Impressions You Want to Create

You can reinforce the impressions you want to create as an interviewer through verbal and nonverbal strategies. First, you need to decide what impressions you want to create. Most participants in interviewing seminars say they want to be perceived as friendly, knowledgeable professionals. To achieve this impression, you need to use your interpersonal skills to establish rapport with the candidate.

Because many of the candidates you interview will not receive job offers but may have other relationships with your company (as customers, for example), you need to create a positive, professional impression.[9] Because both verbal and nonverbal cues create impressions, you need to monitor both what you say and how you say it. Nonverbal cues include dress, gestures, facial expressions, vocal qualities, and eye contact. Guidelines for creating positive, professional impressions are listed in Exhibit 5.2.

Strategy 5: Manage the Interviewing Environment

The first step in managing the environment is to remove all distractions, both auditory and visual, so that each party can easily communicate with the other. Make sure you put yourself in the

---

Exhibit 5.2. Guidelines for Managing Impressions in the Interview

- Dress professionally.
- Show a genuine interest in the interviewees through facial expressions and appropriate verbal responses.
- Smile and call the candidate by name when you say hello.
- Maintain a professional demeanor throughout the interview as you ask questions and probe for behaviors.
- Maintain frequent eye contact with the interviewee even though you're taking notes.
- Avoid behaviors such as excessive head nodding, frowning, or blank stares that can be confusing to interviewees.

candidate's shoes as you review the effectiveness of the environment for interviews within your company. Exhibit 5.3 lists some guidelines for managing the environment in which you conduct your interviews. Each of the guidelines facilitates rather than blocks communication.

Strategy 6: Streamline the Interview Process with Team Interviews

One strategy for dealing with the duplication of multiple interviews and making them less exhausting for the candidate is to conduct a team interview. A team interview (sometimes called a panel interview) involves having several people interview the candidate as a group. Typically, team interviews should be limited to four to five interviewers since more than that number can be intimidating and hard to coordinate.

Team interviews are typically done as the second interview in a selection process. There is no need to involve multiple interviewers unless the candidate passes an initial screening by

---

Exhibit 5.3. Guidelines for Managing the Interview Environment

- Choose a quiet environment free of distractions.
- Choose an environment with a comfortable temperature and soft lighting.
- Provide comfortable seating for both parties.
- Establish a distance between you and the candidate that facilitates communication.
- Establish an angle for the seating that allows eye contact but does not place the candidate directly across a table or desk from the interviewer.
- Reduce distractions (interruptions, ringing phones, intriguing documents, computer screens, outside noise). Many experienced interview subjects can read text upside down quite easily, so put away anything that might divert attention from the interview.
- Reduce barriers (cluttered desks, intimidating seating arrangements) that inhibit communication during an interview. Consider using a round table, if feasible, to minimize power differences between the parties.

demonstrating some potential for the job. Team interviews are also more effective for higher position levels, higher levels of technical competence, and jobs that involve interacting with multiple constituencies. However, some organizations that are very team oriented demonstrate their commitment to teams by using team interviews to select even entry-level workers.

In addition to reducing the duplication and exhaustion of back-to-back interviews, team interviews can make interviewing more accurate. One reason for this is that the interviewers have the same set of questions and answers to use as the basis for their assessment of the candidate. Additionally, interviewers involved in the team interview are more likely to challenge each other regarding the basis for their assessment. The possibility of being challenged causes interviewers to carefully consider the reasons for their hiring decisions and to use a more objective standard. However, when team interviewers use a subjective decision process, research shows that team interviews do not predict performance better than individual interviews.[10]

There are several benefits to team interviews beyond their ability to predict performance expectations. Team interviews can also be an unobtrusive way to train interviewers to interview more effectively. A single interview typically takes place in the privacy of an individual office. People who can see how their colleagues conduct interviews have a chance to learn from that experience. Team interviews can make it easier for better interviewers to pass on tips to weaker ones. Team interviews can also be a mechanism for identifying those individuals who need additional interviewer training.

Perhaps the biggest benefit of the team interview is what it says to candidates. Many organizations say they are committed to the team process, but run candidates through separate interviews one at a time. The team interview says, "We walk the talk." As one candidate said when asked about team interviews: "As they are interviewing me, I'm trying to evaluate them. I'm impressed by companies that use the team interview process, since it tells me they live their philosophy." In a team interview the applicant gets the opportunity to see how the people who will be important on the job interact. As another applicant noted, "I was involved in a team interview where it was quite clear that the interviewers did not get along. I'm not sure that I would have picked that up in a one-on-one interview. I knew I would not be happy there."

We have heard people object that team interviews are more stressful than individual interviews, but we believe that comparing the anxiety of a team interview to one individual interview is the wrong comparison. Team interviews do not eliminate all the individual interviews, but they do reduce the number. As a result, instead of six or seven hour-long, back-to-back interviews, a candidate may go through just an individual interview followed by a team interview and then perhaps another individual interview at the end of the process. Which of these alternatives would you find more stressful? Most of the candidates we have talked to say they prefer the team interview process, combined with fewer individual interviews. As one candidate said, "I just like to get it done."

CHAPTER SUMMARY

In this chapter, we have discussed strategies for conducting effective interviews. We reviewed the typical problems—unstructured or poorly structured interviews, environmental distractions, and multiple back-to-back interviews—that lead to poorly conducted interviews. Strategies for conducting effective interviews that we presented include developing and using an interviewer guide, previewing the interview process, probing to gather more complete behavioral data, reinforcing the impressions you want to create, managing the interviewing environment, and streamlining the interview process with team interviews. Guidelines for implementing the various strategies were described. In the next chapter, we will explore the process that takes place after all interviewing is completed—making the hiring decision.

In the following "Perspectives," three managers describe the benefits of using an interviewer guide to conduct interviews in their organizations. A vice president of human resources also describes how interviewers use behavioral probing and the challenges and benefits of team interviewing.

Perspectives on Conducting Effective Interviews

Mike Johnson, Human Resources Manager, Plante & Moran

What are the benefits of developing and using an Interviewer Guide?

Because of our style of interviewing, we interview all candidates against a standard for our company. We do not ask our interviewers to ask the same questions for every candidate, but we ask them to ask questions from the same categories so we make sure that we are assessing people across the range of their talents. Each interviewer has some freedom to choose some questions within the categories.

We have not always used an Interviewer Guide. We implemented one about five years ago. We believe it has enhanced our consistency. However, having a guide is not enough. You have to be sure that the guide has the right questions or you can be consistently bad. You have to make sure that your interviewers have the conceptual understanding of why they are asking the questions. The guide should have both the questions and sample answers so that people understand what you are getting at in asking the questions. I think the guide has had a positive impact, but I do not think it would have had as much of an impact if our interviewers were not made aware why these questions are important and what they are trying to measure.

Susan J. Adams, Chief of Recruitment, International Monetary Fund

What are the benefits of developing and using an Interviewer Guide?

In the past, we would have asked questions in a fairly random manner. Now each of the team panelists is assigned a segment of the questioning, with all panelists allowed to probe with follow-ups. This has made the interview much more orderly (less randomized) and has allowed us to compare answers much more easily across candidates. The "flow" of the interview is always a little rougher with the first candidate in the chair, but by the second or third candidate, the panel works seamlessly.

We have always offered a laminated, customized "IMF Pocket Guide for Interviewers" to our line managers, but it only had general information about the types of questions to avoid. The new Interviewer Guide includes the general script of the interview, and this has helped direct the flow better.

Susan Mason, Vice President of Human Resources,
Old Kent Financial Services

What are the benefits of developing and using an Interviewer Guide?

The Interviewer Guide has several benefits for Old Kent Financial Services. First, developing the guide helped us focus on matching the job-specific behavior with the appropriate question that targets that behavior. Second, the guide assists us in keeping the interview on track by having prepared questions as well as the desired or effective answer. Finally, the guide provides a standard set of questions for all candidates, which helps protect the organization against any perception of discrimination.

How do interviewers use behavioral probing in interviews at Old Kent Financial Services?

It takes a while for interviewers to get used to behavioral probing because it can be uncomfortable at first. Some candidates seem almost physically uncomfortable with the probing technique because their examples may be too weak or they lack the necessary experience. You feel like you just keep asking, "Then what do you do?" If the candidate provides a quality answer and you probe, they generally respond positively because you are "guiding" them toward the information that you need. The value has been the quality of information we collect. With stronger information, the hiring decision becomes easier.

What are the challenges and benefits of using team interviews?

Team interviewing requires far more coordination among the interviewers than scheduling multiple back-to-back interviews. Team interviewing also requires preparation to define roles, types of questions each participant will ask, interviewing styles, and the general logistics of the interview. Creating core teams of interviewers (groups who often interview as a unit) has streamlined our process and created a more seamless interview for the candidate.

Applications

1. What strategies do you use to structure your interviews?
2. How do you manage the interviewing environment so that you communicate effectively with the interviewee?
3. What strategies can you use to improve your ability to probe the interviewee's responses for behaviors that demonstrate the desired performance expectations?
4. What are the impressions you are trying to create as you conduct your interviews? What strategies do you use to create those impressions?
5. What are the benefits of using team interviews in your organization? What strategies lead to effective team interviews?

Making the Hiring Decision

I nterviewers often focus on what questions to ask and how to ask them, with little emphasis on how to use the information gathered during the interview. Making the hiring decision, probably the most important part of the interview process, receives less attention from interviewers than other parts of the interviewing process. People seem to be operating under the assumption that selection errors are a function of the failure to gather the right type and depth of information about the candidate. Although inadequate data gathering does contribute to failures in hiring, other important contributors are actions that interviewers take or fail to take when making the final hiring decision.

Complete Assessment 6.1. As you do so, think about the process you used to make the decision to hire or not to hire the person you interviewed most recently.

In this chapter, we will explain why the actions listed in Assessment Statements 1, 2, and 4 can lead to poor hiring decisions. We will begin by discussing the link between the interviewing data you gather and the behavioral predictions you should make to reach a hiring decision. We will also describe sources of poor decisions and recommend strategies to deal with them. Finally, we suggest the contributions that a structured decision-making process makes to recruiting and retaining good people. By taking appropriate actions when making hiring decisions, interviewers can significantly improve the climate for managing employee performance, which in turn leads to better retention.

■ Assessment 6.1. ■
Assessing Your Decision Process

1. During the interview, I decided that I would hire or not hire the candidate.
   ☐ Agree   ☐ Disagree

2. I made my decision without reviewing the candidate's comments related to each of my performance expectations.
   ☐ Agree   ☐ Disagree

3. After completing the interview, I could predict the types of specific actions the candidate would demonstrate in the key areas of the job.
   ☐ Agree   ☐ Disagree

4. I knew intuitively that the candidate would fit in my organization.
   ☐ Agree   ☐ Disagree

5. While reviewing the candidate's résumé, I did not reach a conclusion as to whether this person would be a very good or very poor employee.
   ☐ Agree   ☐ Disagree

■ Linking the Interviewing Data to a Behavioral Decision

Strategic interviewing not only links questions and responses to the desired performance expectations, it also links answers to behavioral decision making. After the interview, the interviewer uses the resulting data to make behavioral predictions about how the candidate will perform in the job. For example, if you are looking for an employee who will work as an internal consultant with groups that have especially diverse needs, the questions you ask in the interview should lead to information that you can use to predict how the candidate will deal with conflicting demands and requirements.

Research has shown that a structured process in conducting an interview improves decision quality.[1] A structured behavioral approach in the hiring decision will also improve quality. Four steps describe a structured process for making hiring decisions:

1. Review the performance expectations.
2. Detail and review the candidate's actions and behaviors.
3. Compare the actions and behaviors against the performance expectations.
4. Make a behavioral prediction about the candidate's future behavior in relation to the job context and performance expectations.

Following the strategies we have outlined in Chapters Three and Four will yield the data required for the first two steps. In Step 2 interviewers are essentially describing what the person has done. Once this is clear, they can move to Step 3, a careful analysis of the match between each of the candidate's competencies described through actions and behaviors and the job's specific requirements. Basically, interviewers are asking,

"Do the candidate's behaviors meet, exceed, or fail to meet expectations?" The answers that were prepared prior to the interview should be the standard for making this judgment. Interviewers should reach their conclusions by comparing the candidate's answers to the sample responses that describe different levels of the performance expectations.

Steps 2 and 3 can be thought of as "What did the candidate do?" and "So what does it mean?" Step 4 is "What predictions can be made about the candidate's future behaviors?" In Step 4, interviewers look at the data to decide whether the candidate's separate actions combine to meet the performance expectations for the job. In essence, Step 4 also asks the question, "How do we combine and weigh the various performance expectations to reach an overall decision on the candidate?" The decision is based on behavioral predictions of the candidate's future performance. Interviewers are predicting the strengths the candidate is likely to demonstrate on the job as well as areas of needed development. The final part of this analysis involves verifying that the predicted behaviors match the hiring manager's expectations for the new employee.

■ Problems That Lead to Poor Decision Making

Many factors affect the quality of the hiring decision, but three key problems inevitably lead to poor results. Probably the most common problem is reliance on personal reactions and impressions. A second problem is using the candidates to set the level of standards for the hiring decision. A third is focusing on incomplete or non–job-related information rather than on the connection between the candidate's job-related competencies and the performance expectations. Upcoming sections discuss each of these problems.

Relying on Personal Reactions and Impressions

In earlier chapters, we argued that a good hiring decision starts with how you prepare for the interview. If you cannot define success, you will not be able to measure it. Interviewers who do not define what they are looking for fall back on personal reactions or impressions because they have no other basis for deciding. They tend to focus on the candidate's personal characteristics or interpersonal style.

Since personal reactions are usually not connected to performance expectations, an interviewer's personal reactions are unlikely to predict future success on the job. The interviewer may like the candidate because of comfortable communication in the interview, but the interviewer will not have valid reasons for the hiring decision.

Subjective impressions lead to subjective decisions. For example, some interviewers say they are looking for someone who can "fit with the culture" or who has "the right kind of personality." Although these labels may refer to important factors that will influence effective job performance, the labels are fundamentally subjective and undefined. When interviewers do not objectively define the specific behaviors they need to look for to verify the candidate can "fit with the culture" or has "the right personality," they risk falling into the *similar-to-me* error.[2] This error occurs when the interviewer makes a judgment based on similar background or experiences. Clearly, selecting a new employee because the person is like you will have little to do with the candidate's ability to do the job.

You can like someone who has very little competency to do a specific job. Likewise, you can work very well with someone you would not consider as a close friend. We are not saying that interviewers should hire people they dislike, but we are suggesting that "like" or "dislike" should be connected to what people do at work and how they do it.

Some interviewers say they rely on their "gut feelings." This happens when an interviewer has a strong personal reaction that the candidate is qualified or unqualified for the job, without being able to substantiate the reason for that reaction. The interviewer's gut feeling may be a signal that the interviewer believes the candidate will not meet some aspect of the performance expectations required for a particular job. In either case, personal impressions or gut feelings on their own are not likely to lead to high-quality hiring decisions.

Using the Candidates to Set the Level of Standards

Even if the interviewer does not focus on personal impressions, another typical judgment error can occur if the interviewer relies on the candidates to set the level of standards for the hiring decision. At some point in the decision process, interviewers must determine a standard to make their hiring decision. Interviewers who do not define their standards prior to conducting the interview are likely to hire based on what's called a *contrast error*. A contrast error occurs when an interviewer compares candidates against each other, rather than comparing each against the job requirements. After interviewing several candidates, the interviewer may decide that candidate X is more likable and has more skills than candidates Y and Z. While these can be valid personal reactions to the candidate, they are not valid reasons to hire. Candidate X's skills still should be compared to the performance expectations for the job.

As we discussed in Chapter Four, the interviewer who judges the quality of the answers based on the best answer in the applicant pool is ignoring what is needed to meet performance expectations. Again, a contrast error occurs because the comparison is made solely between the applicants' responses. Instead, comparison should be between each applicant's responses and an objective standard. With the appropriate comparison, the interviewer avoids the problem of an unqualified candidate appearing qualified due to the lower qualifications of the applicant pool.

Using Incomplete or Non-Job-Related Data

The problems discussed in preceding sections were about not knowing what to look for. Another problem relates to using incomplete or non-job-related data when making the hiring decision.[3] *Stereotyping* is a judgment error that occurs when an interviewer makes assumptions that certain behaviors will or will not occur because of other characteristics of the candidate. For example, a candidate with an engineering degree might be perceived by an interviewer to be unable to interact effectively with a wide range of people, simply because the candidate is an engineer. The evidence for this conclusion is the dubious stereotype that all engineers have weak interpersonal skills. The evidence is not any specific behaviors the candidate exhibits or discusses.

Positive stereotyping can also lead to hiring errors. For example, a corporate vice president mistakenly assumed a candidate for a sales position could respond effectively to customer questions simply because the candidate had worked for a prestigious organization. Another example is the practice of hiring graduates from top-rated universities on the assumption that the graduates will be successful in a job solely because they attended a prestigious school.

Sometimes interviewers use only a portion of the relevant data gathered about the candidate in making the comparison to the performance expectation. Consequently, an interviewer may overgeneralize that a person will be effective or ineffective across a number of areas based on behavior in one area. For example, you might assume that the candidate who is technically skilled will also be a good manager of technical employees by virtue of that technical expertise.

If interviewers assume that a candidate's technical expertise in one area extends to other, different areas, they are making a judgment based on a *halo error.* Halo errors typically occur when interviewers are hiring someone to respond to a number of technical needs, some of which are easier to fill than others. For example, a manager may be hiring someone to program in the computer language Java (a relatively common skill), but may also need the person to work with less common languages. A manager who assumes that Java competency extends to those other software languages is making a halo error.

An interviewer who gathers non–job-related information is apt to emphasize this irrelevant data when making the hiring decision. Also, how the interviewer records the information in written notes can inappropriately influence the hiring decision. For example, the interviewer's notes might stress that the candidate enjoys skydiving on weekends. If the hiring manager decides to reject the candidate, assuming that the candidate's dangerous hobby may lead to high-risk behavior on the job, the candidate is rejected for non–job-related reasons. When irrelevant information or non–job-related data is gathered and recorded, the quality of the hiring decision declines.

In summary, interviewers often collect incomplete or wrong types of information, and even when the information is correct, do not use it appropriately in making the decision. These problems are partially attributable to a lack of knowledge and motivation on the part of the interviewer. Interviewers often do not know what to ask, but they also are not given many incentives to use the right data in making their decisions.

■ Strategies for Making Better Hiring Decisions

To avoid the problems that lead to poor hiring decisions, interviewers need to take a more disciplined approach to decision making. The recommendations we provide in this section are designed to both educate and motivate interviewers and organizations to make better hiring decisions.

Strategy 1: Gather Appropriate Information to Support or Refute Gut Feelings

If you have a gut feeling about a candidate's ability to do the job, you should verify whether your feeling is related to performance expectations. Stated another way, a gut feeling is an unasked question. When you feel the candidate cannot meet the job's performance expectations, you have to gather the information from the candidate to support or refute your gut feeling.

The first thing to do is ask yourself, "What is the basis for my gut feeling?" Is there something that the candidate said or did not say? Do you think that the candidate is withholding information from you? Do you think the candidate is exaggerating the quality or depth of past experiences? Do you think the candidate is not being truthful? By exploring the basis for your feeling, you are focusing more objectively on the candidate's behaviors.

The second question you can ask yourself is "What do my feelings suggest about how the candidate will act on the job?" This question requires you to examine whether your gut feeling is related to performance expectations. If it is, you need to ask about the performance expectation that is the basis for your gut feeling. For example, if you feel the candidate is not sharing information with you and you conclude that this may be someone who is generally uncooperative with others, ask the candidate, "What examples from your past demonstrate your cooperation with another individual or department? What were the results?"

Another strategy is to gather job-related information from the candidate's references to support or refute your gut feeling. Although many references today will supply only dates of employment, some references are willing to answer questions about the candidate's job behaviors. In our previous example, a reference could help you determine if the candidate is uncooperative with others or simply strongly introverted in new situations.

Interviewers should be very cautious in relying on gut feelings. Many gut feelings result from differences in communication styles. Sharp contrasts in the way individuals communicate can lead to misperceptions if the interviewer is not consciously aware that the person's communication style is just different.[4] Following the Strategic Interviewing Approach will reduce the possibility of gut feelings' influencing your hiring decisions. Instead, you will focus on gathering job-related information to predict job performance.

Strategy 2: Use a Structured Approach to Document Your Hiring Decision Process

Interviewers need to look carefully at the data they have gathered before they make a decision. We recommend asking them to state the basis for their assessment in writing. Part 1 of Exhibit 6.1 is a sample form based on the four steps we described in the beginning of this chapter for linking interviewing data to the hiring decision. This form can be used to formally score the candidate's interview and document your hiring decision process. The instructions on the form ask for assessments focused on performance expectations.

For each performance expectation assessed in Column 1, first make sure that the meaning of the expectation is clear. For team interviews, this might involve a brief discussion to ensure there is agreement among all the team members on what each expectation means.

In Column 2, you list and review the candidate's key actions and behaviors related to each expectation. Use descriptive, not evaluative, language. For example, a description such as "influences others by gathering data and using research to support arguments" will verify a performance expectation related to influencing others. Evaluative language, which is less effective, might indicate that you thought the candidate was "a strong salesperson," or "can handle any situation." Descriptive language will allow you to be specific about the competencies the candidate has or does not have for the job.

To clarify the relative importance of performance expectations, you can designate performance expectations as either essential or desirable. Essential performance expectations are those that a candidate must demonstrate in order to meet the job requirements. Desirable performance expectations are not required but advantageous for the success of the new employee. If a hiring manager considers all the performance expectations essential, you still need to prioritize them to weigh their relative importance in predicting the future success of the new employee. Determining the priorities of the performance expectations should occur as you prepare the interview. Otherwise, if you wait until the decision stage of the process, you can be unduly influenced by the candidate's responses. You can end up selecting an employee who cannot meet all of your essential performance expectations because of strengths in one particular area.

Part 2 of Exhibit 6.1 helps you organize the material in Part 1 to get an overall picture of how the candidate is likely to perform on the job. This structured decision approach puts the key issues in front of the interviewer. It increases the chances that the interviewer will indeed use the correct information to predict a candidate's future job performance. It also creates an important paper trail that can be used to assess and improve the decision-making process. This documentation can be a valuable reminder for both educating the interviewers and motivating them to use the right information.

Using the assessment form can have other positive benefits for managers and organizations. First, it can help them create a more effective socialization process for the new hire. Using a

Exhibit 6.1. Candidate Assessment Form

Name of applicant_____   Interviewer_____   Date Interviewed_____

Part 1

Instructions: Part 1

Follow these steps in order for each performance expectation assessed.

Column 1: State the performance expectation. Make sure that everyone involved in making the decision agrees to the definition.

Column 2: Describe the candidate's behaviors that demonstrate the performance expectation. Remember to describe and not judge at this step.

Column 3: Use the sample answers from the interviewer guide and compare columns 1 and 2 to rate whether the candidate's behaviors fail to
meet expectations (rating=0), meets expectations (rating=1), or exceeds expectations (rating=2).

Column 4: Briefly explain the reason for your rating in Column 3.

Column 1: Performance Expectations (List in order of importance to the job. Include goals, job barriers, and competency requirements.)	Column 2: Candidate Behaviors Relevant to the Performance Expectation	Column 3: Ratings of the Candidate 0=below expectations, 1=meets expectations, 2=exceeds expectations	Column 4: Reasons for the Ratings in Column 3
Performance expectation 1:			
Performance expectation 2:			

Part 2

Instructions: Part 2

1. Using the information from Part 1, summarize how the candidate is likely to meet performance expectations as well as the development that may be needed.

2. Based on this review, rate the overall level of this candidate's likely job performance (0=below expectations, 1=meets expectations, 2=exceeds expectations).

Strengths: Specific things that the candidate should be able to do well on the job.	Areas for Development: Areas or actions that are not likely to meet expectations.	Overall Rating of Candidate: 0 = below expectations 1 = meets expectations 2 = exceeds expectations

summary of the candidate's strengths in Part 2, hiring managers can identify assignments in which new hires can use their strengths and are more likely to succeed, thus starting a cycle of "success breeds success." Managers can also use the information described under "Areas for Development" to target new employees' early training. With targeted training, the new employees will get up to speed more quickly. The same information can also be shared with the new hires, so that they also can take corrective steps quickly. Perhaps most important overall, the information in the form clarifies performance expectations that can help new hires understand better what is needed to be successful on the job.

Strategy 3: Review the Decision Process and Outcome

Do quality control procedures govern the important decisions that your organization makes? Most managers would say that they do. They try to ensure that key decisions on important issues are not overlooked and the right process is used. In every organization, some jobs are key to the success of the organization. At a minimum, the hiring process and the hiring decisions for these key jobs should be reviewed before the decision is finalized and the job is offered.

One reason for reviewing hiring processes and decisions is to avoid the practice or appearance of discrimination. Interviewers may treat all candidates the same and use the same decision criteria, but the outcome of their decisions may still adversely affect certain groups. For example, an interviewer may be disproportionately rejecting people over forty, or individuals of a particular ethnic background. This interviewer may be violating discrimination laws by using an interviewing approach that is not based on job-related information.[5] Even if candidates from a protected group (for example, people over forty or minorities) are being rejected for job-related reasons, the organization and the interviewer need to know that such rejection is occurring. This is particularly true for organizations that are making a good-faith effort to achieve a diverse group of employees. Thus the first part of a review of your hiring process should be an analysis of the type of candidates accepted or rejected by interviewers across time.

The more in-depth review would examine the content of interviewing data and the decision process. The first objective would be to make sure that the appropriate information was used correctly in the decision process. One way to conduct this part of the review is to audit the assessment forms used to make hiring decisions. If you used a form similar to Part 1 of Exhibit 6.1, you could audit your process by addressing these questions about the basic information:

- Are the performance expectations clearly defined?
- Are specific behaviors identified?
- Are the behaviors listed in Column 2 appropriate for demonstrating the specific competency requirements?
- Does Column 4 make it clear why the examples cited are rated at their specific level?

There is also the question of whether or not the correct decision was made from the data. You can answer this question by reviewing information collected from Part 2 of the form. You might ask yourself:

- Are there clear descriptions of the predictions of the candidate's future job behaviors? Is there a clear picture of how the candidate is likely to perform in the job?
- Is there a clear connection between what the candidate said in the interview and what is predicted about the candidate's

future performance? Is there a clear connection between the behaviors documented in the assessment and the predicted strengths and areas of development?

- Are the same priorities for essential performance expectations that were set before the interview still used in the decision process? If not, why not? Is this change appropriate?

This type of review process has several benefits. First, the old saying that what gets evaluated gets done really does apply here. Interviewers who know that their assessment will be reviewed are less likely to use non–job-related data and more likely to use job-related information.[6] The result will be better hiring decisions. Second, if reviews are shared with the managers who helped to complete the forms, the feedback can help them manage the people they hire. As hiring managers improve their ability to measure performance, they become not only better at selection but also at other aspects of managing performance such as defining training needs, delegating assignments, and providing feedback. Finally, aggregated reviews of information can be used to select who should be conducting interviews as well as to understand and to assess the effectiveness of the organization's interviewing process.

Who should do the review? And will a review unnecessarily lengthen the hiring process? It is easiest to have the hiring manager's direct supervisor be responsible for reviewing the documents, but some organizations charge this work to a committee of trained individuals. Either option is acceptable as long as the criteria used in the review are clearly defined and communicated to everyone involved in the selection decision.

Regarding the length of the hiring process when review precedes the final decision, speed of hiring can certainly affect an organization's ability to attract and retain good people. However, a review process will not necessarily lengthen the time needed to make every hiring decision. For example, a sample of decisions could be reviewed rather than all decisions. It may not be necessary to intensively review the quality of selection decisions for entry-level jobs that do not require many skills because there may not be much to assess in either the interview or the decision process.

Decisions could be reviewed after the fact. For example, managers may be allowed to make their hiring decision and then submit the form for review afterward. If such a follow-up review reveals problems with the decision process, that manager might be required to submit paperwork prior to making the decision on the next hire. The key issue is not that all decisions are reviewed, but that interviewers know their individual decisions may be reviewed.

Despite the fact that selection decisions are critical to the continued success of a company and have high potential costs in industry, the selection of new employees has gone largely unmonitored. Part of the reason for this neglect is the perception that managers should be allowed to choose the people they work with. While we generally agree with this statement, we believe it is incomplete. To make that thought complete, you need to add to the end of the statement "as long as they use job-related information to make the decision and demonstrate how the candidate is likely to perform on the job."

Monitoring a process does not take away the hiring manager's freedom, it simply increases accountability. Given the importance of selecting good people and the other positive benefits of managers' using the information from hiring decisions, we think it is time to move to making sure that the decision process includes job-related, behavior-specific predictions.

Strategy 4: Use Team Interviews Where Feasible and Appropriate

In Chapter Five we discussed many benefits of team interviews. Team interviews can improve a hiring decision because the team members share their perceptions of an interview in which they all participated. To be effective, team discussion should begin by verifying that all team members agree on what each performance expectation means. They should also agree that the description of the candidate's behavior is an accurate reflection of the candidate's statements in the interview. Only after there is agreement on these issues should the team discuss how the candidate's behaviors and actions compared with performance expectations.

One challenge to good decision making is ensuring that all the interviewers have the right data. Team interviewers typically report they can listen better since they are not solely responsible for asking the next question or probing the candidate's answer. As a result, each interviewer is able to gather more information. Also, with multiple note takers and the opportunity to review differences in notes, the quality of information available for the decision is enhanced.

Additionally, team interviews can improve the motivation of interviewers to use the appropriate information for the hiring decision. Team members often challenge their colleagues to give good reasons for their assessments. This focus on providing a strong rationale and supporting evidence reduces the tendency to rely on gut feelings.

Not all team interviews will produce positive outcomes.[7] Just putting people together to conduct an interview does not necessarily lead to a high-quality decision. Effective team interviews require the same preparation we discussed in Chapters Two through Four. Moreover, status differences or differences in personality can lead one individual to dominate the decision process. If the dominant team member is not using an objective decision process, the hiring decision may not be satisfactory.

To decrease the influence of a dominant team member who is not contributing to the quality of the decision, the team of interviewers can use an anonymous ballot to get initial differences in perception on the table and entered into discussion.[8] Another strategy is to have someone facilitate, ensuring equal input from all team members.

■ The Impact of Effective Decision Making on Recruitment and Retention

Throughout this book, we have emphasized that effective selection through Strategic Interviewing can influence an organization's ability to attract and retain good people. Although the effect may be clearer in the actions you take to prepare for a strategic interview, the decision process can also have a major influence on recruitment and retention. Regarding recruitment, including and using better information in the decision process should expand the pool of acceptable candidates.

As discussed in Chapter One, untrained interviewers often look for a reason to reject a candidate. This reason can be very subjective. For example, interviewers may be looking for candidates who fit with the organization. If they define *fit* subjectively, they may focus on finding someone they like. This approach tends to exclude more potential candidates than a more objective approach would. If interviewers measure fit by first defining the behaviors that the employee should demonstrate, they will focus on finding someone who can behave in a manner that is consistent with the organization's culture. Because this approach uses a more objective process, interviewers are likely to rely on criteria that more candidates can meet. This in turn leads to a bigger pool of candidates.

The process for making hiring decisions can also be a way of differentiating the organization. High-quality individuals are typically interested and motivated by an opportunity to enhance their skills. At the end of the interview process, candidates should be informed of the nature of the decision process. Tell candidates you will be assessing how their strengths match the performance expectations for the job. Candidates will know that if they are offered the job, the organization is interested in their skills. This approach also sends the message that the organization is enhancing the performance of its workforce.

While many factors influence the retention of new employees, the relationship of new employees with their first manager or supervisor can be very important. The process we have described helps to build that relationship by focusing the manager's attention on using appropriate information in assessing and selecting the new hire. As we have noted, good performance data about a worker is useful not only to the person or team making the selection decision but also to managers later on as they delegate, train, assess performance, and provide feedback to the employee. All other things being equal, high-quality employees should seek out this type of situation, since it allows them to develop important skills.

CHAPTER SUMMARY

In this chapter, we began by discussing the link between the interviewing data you gather and the behavioral predictions you should make to reach a hiring decision. We also identified problems that lead to poor hiring decisions. One common problem occurs when interviewers rely on personal reactions and impressions instead of behavioral predictions. Other problems include using the candidates to set the level of standards for the hiring decision and relying on incomplete or non–job-related information to make decisions.

Strategies for making good hiring decisions include gathering appropriate information to support or refute gut feelings, using a structured approach to document your hiring decision process, reviewing both hiring decisions and processes, and using team interviews where it is appropriate. Using all of these strategies can significantly improve the quality of hiring decisions.

The following "Perspectives" illustrate how three organizations are making hiring decisions today based on behavioral predictions. The managers also describe the benefits of making hiring decisions based on more than a gut feeling.

Perspectives on Hiring Decisions

Mike Johnson, Human Resources Manager, Plante & Moran

How do the hiring decisions you make today differ from previous decisions? What are the effects of your approach on hiring decisions? What strategies do you use to monitor and motivate interviewers to make effective decisions?

One sign that the program is working well is that the interviewers can describe the basis for their decisions and they are using the information that we defined as the key criteria for success. In the past, we saw comments on their interviewing forms like "Great candidate," "Bring him in as soon as possible," and so on. The decisions we made were a gut feel for what we thought was going to be a successful person. Today, we make decisions based on key criteria that strategically drive the success of our company.

We motivate our interviewers by including goals related to strategic interviewing as a part of our performance management system. Specifically, achieving these interviewing goals will improve their bonuses. Some of these goals are quality oriented. This drives interviewers to make effective decisions based on the criteria we've set for success.

We have done some team interviews with two interviewers to monitor the quality of our interviewers. When we do this, we have found that we have to have both interviewers talking—not one talking and the other completely quiet. The candidate needs to be at ease with both interviewers. Prior to the interview one member of the team takes responsibility as the lead interviewer so that you don't waste your time in the interview and trip over each other's questions.

Susan J. Adams, Chief of Recruitment, International Monetary Fund

How do the hiring decisions you make today differ from previous decisions? What are the effects of your approach on hiring decisions?

In the past, team hiring decisions were made in a fairly ad hoc fashion. The majority view of the three panelists prevailed, without any systematic scoring or cross-comparison of candidates' responses to the same questions. In some cases, the teams were not even asking the same questions across interviews! Today, our decision process is much more clearcut and the panelists have greater confidence that the "right" candidate has been selected.

Our staff is largely quantitative in nature. The scoring of acceptable answers appeals much more directly to their "comfort with numbers" than the old system of "what's your gut feeling about this candidate?" The old approach was much too "touchy-feely" for these people.

We have always used team or panel interviews and we continue to believe this is the *only* way to interview—but we have further improved the functioning of these panels with the approach and a better preparation of the interviews.

Susan Mason, Vice President of Human Resources,
Old Kent Financial Services

How do the hiring decisions you make today differ from previous decisions? What are the effects of your approach on hiring decisions?
Today, hiring managers using the Strategic Interviewing Approach are more analytical in their decision making process. Rather than relying on that emotion, they have more solid information they can use to make the decision. The question they ask themselves has become "Can this candidate do this job?" rather than "Do I like this candidate?" The core competencies allow the interviewer to realistically evaluate multiple candidates side by side and visualize how successful they would be in this job.

Applications

1. What is the current process that you use to make a selection decision from interviewing data?
2. What do you do to make sure that you are gathering the right information and using it appropriately?
3. How do you make sure that you avoid judgments based on stereotyping, halo, similar-to-me, and contrast errors?
4. What strategies do you use to review and monitor interviewers' decisions?
5. Do you monitor whether your selection decisions produce adverse impact?

Getting Strategic Interviewing to Work for You

Over the years we have trained many individuals in the Strategic Interviewing Approach. As people learn about the process, they have questions about how they should develop and conduct their interviews. Often, people who have been interviewing for a number of years have many of the same questions that new interviewers have. The answers that we give to most of these questions about the Strategic Interviewing Approach have been addressed in our discussion of the six-step approach in the preceding chapters.

Some questions that seminar participants ask as they learn this approach to interviewing are not connected with a particular step in the process but relate to the overall process. Typically, these are questions of implementation. In this chapter, we will answer those questions. We will also identify the signs of success that will let you know that you are making the best use of the Strategic Interviewing Approach.

■ Questions About Implementing Strategic Interviewing

As you read each of the following questions, think about whether this is a concern you have. Consider whether this concern only applies to Strategic Interviewing or whether you have had this concern with other interviewing processes that you are using or have used in the past.

Does Strategic Interviewing Take Too Long?

Consider how much time you spend on replacing people who are not good employees or who quit unexpectedly. Also take into account the time you spend on individuals who lack the skills for their jobs. Compare this time you are already spending with an estimate of the time you can save by having an effective selection process that reduces turnover. How much time could you save by clarifying performance standards before you hire so that performance appraisals, coaching and counseling, and determining training needs can be accomplished more effectively? The time you are currently spending on coaching and replacing ineffective employees and the time you will save hiring good employees will vary. It will depend on the specifics of your situation—the type of jobs you are trying to fill, your turnover rates, and the availability of candidates for the position.

Many of the people we have trained and who are using Strategic Interviewing have told us that they save time interviewing with this approach, particularly with jobs they fill on a regular basis. They say the time is invested up front in developing an interviewer guide with clearly stated performance expectations along with questions and possible answers linked to the expectations. Then when a position opens, they can review the prepared interviewer guide and move confidently into the interviews.

Remember that your preparation of an interviewer guide for a specific job is a one-time investment. Unless performance expectations change, the guide that details performance expectations, questions, and possible answers does not need to be changed.

Is Strategic Interviewing Worth My Time and Effort?

Time is a valuable resource, but you need to compare the time you spend to the value you gain in return for the time you invest. If the benefits outweigh the costs, you will be motivated to invest your time and effort in implementing the Strategic Interviewing Approach.

If you believe that time is money, you also need to calculate the costs of turnover as well as the costs of a bad hire in your organization. Replacing employees typically can cost one-third of a new hire's annual salary. Bad hires not only add to turnover costs, they subtract from your productivity and your quality.

On the other hand, think about the value a good performer in a particular job adds to your department or organization beyond what is provided by an average or a poor performer. If you conclude that the value is negligible, you should not be spending your time using Strategic Interviewing for that job. However, if identifying a good employee for a particular job is important to your organization, you should be using this interviewing approach. Most people would agree that selecting the right CEO is worth the time and effort it takes. The same is true for hiring employees with technical expertise or professionals who will have significant responsibilities. Finding an entry-level delivery person might not justify the same investment of time and effort.

When few candidates are available for an open position, most interviewers would probably focus more on recruiting just to be sure that they find someone to hire. The Strategic Interviewing Approach would combine both measuring the candidates and selling the job. Even when there are only a few candidates, you still need to begin with a clear understanding of performance expectations. By measuring the candidate against the performance expectations, you will avoid hiring the person who is the best of your currently limited pool, but who is not likely to be a good hire. As you look at all the jobs between the top-level and the lowest-level positions, the more technical or professional the job, the more value you will gain by spending the time and effort to hire good people.

Do Hiring Managers Resist This Approach to Interviewing?

People we have trained have often expressed the concern that they won't be able to convince hiring managers to use this approach. They believe that hiring managers will be reluctant to give up what they view as their right to hire the person they feel is best for the job. Our experience has been just the opposite. Across a wide range of companies and functional areas, line managers who have been trained in Strategic Interviewing quickly understand the logic of matching candidates to performance expectations and understand the value of a systematic approach to interviewing.

This approach is a new way of interviewing and managers need to understand the rationale behind Strategic Interviewing and the value of the strategies. If managers understand why this approach works and how it compares to the way they typically conduct interviews, they are less likely to resist changing. For many managers today the limited pool of qualified candidates coupled with the high costs of turnover is a compelling argument to improve the way they select new employees.

We have also found that hiring managers are particularly persuaded when they discover the value in developing an integrated performance management system. An integrated performance management system links selection with other human resource processes including performance appraisals, training and development, and coaching. Since many managers have never considered that an interview is an attempt to predict a performance appraisal, they continue to view the performance appraisal process and the interview process as two separate and unrelated events. Perhaps more puzzling, many managers have never considered using the information from one management process to benefit another process. Strategic Interviewing helps managers understand this connection and feel more capable when they conduct interviews. As one hiring manager recently told us, "I now have a process to use that makes sense. I'm not going to have to rely on my gut feelings."

Certainly there are individuals who will resist changing how they interview. Some people enjoy playing the role of a psychologist or using their own unique questioning techniques. But be careful that you are not assuming that you will meet resistance from hiring managers; you may be stereotyping managers as simply reluctant to give up their control over how they hire. The persuasive power of stereotyping was brought home to us in a recent consulting project where we were asked to train the top management team of a Fortune 50 company. We went into the project a bit skeptical that these seasoned executives would be open to modifying their interviewing approaches. Their openness to the process and their willingness to adopt it whole-heartedly proved that our initial skepticism was unfounded. Once hiring managers understand the process, they are typically very committed to it and are not a roadblock to hiring good people.

□

Can Strategic Interviewing Be Implemented with Limited Resources?

This is a question that is often raised by individuals from smaller companies with a limited staff. Typically, the question is raised because the questioner wants to change the company's whole interviewing process and knows the resources are not there to support that kind of change. We caution against making very big and immediate changes. As with any skill, it takes time and effort to master the techniques outlined in this book. Thus we encourage starting with modest changes to develop the skills and build support for the process. Here are some suggestions for implementing Strategic Interviewing with limited resources:

- Start with one job. Select a job for which there are many incumbents and many openings or one with high visibility to create the greatest impact and support for the process.
- Develop questions for one performance expectation. Choose the performance expectation that is most important for a specific open position. Develop questions to assess goals, job barriers, and competency requirements that separate the good performer from the poor performer.
- Work with one hiring manager who understands the process and is likely to be supportive. Ideally work with someone who can be a champion for the process and an advocate to encourage others to adopt and support the process.
- Use team interviews as a way to build understanding and support among a small group of managers. Again, select team members who are likely to be supportive of working together to select new employees and willing to try a new approach.
- Use a cost-benefit analysis to educate others on the costs of turnover and bad hiring. Identify the benefits that can accrue with the Strategic Interviewing Approach as a way of building support for implementing this new approach.

Where Is the Best Place to Begin the Strategic Interviewing Approach?

Ask yourself these two questions: "Where do I need to make the most decisions in selecting people?" and "Where does my selection decision matter the most?" Typically, the best place to start Strategic Interviewing is where you will get the most return for your investment of time and effort. If you are hiring a large number of customer service representatives, you can start implementing Strategic Interviewing by identifying whether there is a difference between a good customer service representative and a poor one. Assuming there is, determining the goals, job barriers, and competency requirements that make up the performance expectations will allow you to develop a standardized interviewer guide for the customer service job. With this systematic, strategic approach for the many interviews you need to conduct, you will save time and, more important, hire good people for the job.

Also, if you are hiring for a position that has few qualified candidates or is key to the success of your department or organization, a strategic approach will allow you to select a candidate that can meet or exceed your expectations. By clearly determining your performance expectations and accurately measuring whether the candidate can meet those expectations, you will avoid simply hiring the best of what's available in the pool. Instead, you probably will find yourself extending your search until you find a candidate that can meet the expectations of the job. Selecting a starting point that leads to positive results reinforces and motivates continued implementation.

Exhibit 7.1 contains a list of activities that participants in our University of Michigan Strategic Interviewing Seminars often cite as the actions they plan to complete after attending the training. These actions are starting points for beginning the implementation process. As you look over the list of action items, consider which items you might use to begin changing your

Exhibit 7.1. **Action Plans for Implementing Strategic Interviewing**

Preparing for a Strategic Interview:
- Gather data to assess if the organization provides an accurate, realistic job preview and how it can be enhanced.
- Manage the interview process by setting goals for each interview.
- Reduce duplication in the process by standardizing the approach in a multiple interview format.
- Use team interviews where possible to cut down the number of back-to-back interviews and to build consensus among key decision makers.
- Define performance expectations that include goals, job barriers, and competency requirements.
- Develop interviewer guides that include questions and sample answers that are connected to performance expectations to increase the accuracy of measurement.
- Provide interviewing training for hiring managers so they understand the strategies and the rationale that supports the strategies.

Conducting a Strategic Interview:
- Use effective communication and listening strategies to create positive, professional impressions with candidates.
- Manage the interview environment to facilitate the communication between the interviewer and the candidate.
- Follow the interviewer guide—use a standard set of questions for all candidates for the same job.
- Use behavioral probing techniques to gather information about the candidate's past behavior as a predictor of future behavior in similar situations.
- Use behavioral probes to examine "red flags" that may signal the candidate will not meet your performance expectations.
- Include hiring managers in team interviews to train them in the Strategic Interviewing Approach.

Making a Selection Decision:
- Focus your hiring decision on whether the candidate meets or exceeds the job's performance expectations.
- Develop an evaluation and decision form to record the reasons for selecting the person to fill the position.
- Review interview decisions and their rationale to monitor the quality of hiring decisions.
- Review interview decisions to assess vulnerability to discrimination complaints.

process and building support for changing the way your organization interviews and selects candidates. The list is divided into steps that you can use in preparing for a strategic interview, conducting the interview, and making the selection decision.

■ Signs of Successful Implementation

While there are a number of possible starting points for implementing the Strategic Interviewing Approach, the best way to quickly see signs of success is to systematically work through the six-step model with a specific job that is open. If you put the time and effort into this process, there are several key indicators of success that will become evident. First and most important, the quality of the people you select should improve. Second, candidates will have more positive impressions of your interviewing process. Third, you will be able to recognize and use the linkages among performance expectations, questions, answers, and the decision process. In turn, you will increase your confidence in your hiring process.

Improvement in the Quality of People You Select

A noticeable improvement in the quality of people you select is the best indicator of successful implementation of this approach. Your new hires should be able to meet or exceed the performance expectations on the job. If you have focused on finding a match between the candidate's competencies and the job's performance expectations, you are much more likely to discover the new employee quickly succeeds on the job. This approach also helps you to identify developmental needs that you can address with coaching or training to help new employees improve their competencies for the job.

When employees quickly succeed on the job, the value they add to your department or organization becomes evident in the brevity of the time they take to learn the job and the immediate contributions they make in areas such as productivity, quality, or creativity. Improved quality in selecting employees also means you will have fewer surprises. Specifically, there should be fewer times when you are fooled into thinking that someone is good who later fails to meet your expectations. Likewise, you should not be surprised that someone turns out to be a much better performer than you expected.

Positive Candidate Impressions

Another sign that Strategic Interviewing is working is that the candidates you interview will have more positive impressions of your organization. Also, they should receive the types of messages you intend to send through the interview process. This sign can be verified with a survey of candidate perceptions of your interview process. An easy way to do this is to use the techniques we mentioned in Chapter Two for measuring candidates' perceptions of the interview process and the messages they infer about the organization from it.

When candidates develop positive impressions based on the interview, they are more likely to accept job offers. Given the difficulty recruiters have filling some open positions today, creating positive impressions that lead to job acceptances is important. High-quality candidates are particularly impressed with an organization that they believe is taking the time and effort to accurately assess their competencies for the job.

Linkages Among Performance Expectations, Questions, Answers, and the Decision Process

You will also know you are succeeding with Strategic Interviewing when you recognize that performance expectations are driving your interview process. By using the linkages among performance expectations, questions, answers, and decisions, you will be gathering information that leads to the selection of a person who can meet or exceed your expectations on the job. Your starting point will be a clear identification of what you want a candidate to do to be effective on the job. To define your performance expectations, you need to specify the goals, job barriers, and competency requirements that the candidate will need to display to meet your expectations. With practice, you will begin to use this information not only to select good candidates, but also to coach, counsel, and evaluate them effectively. You will see a tight connection between the processes you use to select, train, and evaluate your employees. More important, this connection among performance management functions will be clearer to the people who work for you.

When you conduct interviews with a strategic approach, you will no longer accept the candidate's labels as descriptions of behavior. Instead, you will focus your behavioral probing on asking the candidate to detail specific actions taken in the past. Certainly, you will probe the candidate's responses in a manner in which the candidate does not feel interrogated and will actually appreciate your efforts to gather additional information. With this approach, you may still be tempted to rush to judgment—but you will understand why you need to wait until all of the information is in before you assess if the candidate is right for the job.

Perhaps the most subjective indicator that this process is working for you will be your own feelings about the reasoning you use for making a hiring decision. Making decisions based on your gut feelings will seem too subjective. When you do have a gut feeling, you will be able to probe to find the extent to which it is job related. By exploring the source of your concerns, you will have objective, defensible reasons for your selection decision. In your discussions about candidates, you will provide specific examples of actions the candidate has or has not taken. Based on this information, you will make behavioral predictions about how the candidate will perform on the job.

CHAPTER SUMMARY

In this chapter we have answered some of the questions that you may have about implementing the Strategic Interviewing Approach in your own interviews. Also, we have explored the signs that will indicate that you are making this process work for you. Clearly, the most important sign will be the quality of the new employees you add to your department or organization. Second, the positive impressions that you create with candidates will not only encourage your top candidates to accept job offers but will also lead to positive public relations. The people who interview with your company and are not hired will continue to have positive impressions of your organization long after the interview is over. Third, a key indicator that this process is working will occur when you are able to recognize, use, and describe the linkages among performance expectations, questions, answers, and decisions. When you use performance expectations to drive your interview process, you will be more likely to hire employees who will be successful on the job.

Throughout this book we have described a variety of strategies that we have seen work very effectively to enhance the interview process across a variety of levels in a wide range of organizations. We are confident these processes will lead to hiring good people who become good employees.

Keep in mind, a good selection process requires more than an effective interview. There are other important components needed for effective selection, such as accurate reference checking, application processes, and other forms of testing. Interviewing is just one selection technique, but clearly the one that we rely on the most. If you are interested in other ways to enhance your selection process, you need to investigate ways to make more effective use of the other processes available to you. Together these approaches can provide a powerful selection process depending on the needs in your organization. Finally, as you might expect, we also encourage you to enhance your interview process by applying the strategies of this book.

We close with a final set of "Perspectives" from individuals who have successfully implemented the Strategic Interviewing Approach in their organizations. Their experiences underscore the value of strategic interviewing—hiring good people.

Perspectives on Making Strategic Interviewing Work

Mike Johnson, Human Resources Manager, Plante & Moran

What were some of the key changes you made in moving your organization to a Strategic Interviewing Approach?

The first thing you have to do is convince people that this is a better approach to interviewing. A technique that has been very powerful for us is to provide examples of the typical kind of interview process compared to this approach when we train interviewers. This technique sells really well. It doesn't take long for people to see that they have better criteria to make a judgment with Strategic Interviewing. I think interviewers are anxious when they make decisions with a gut feel. Most interviewers understand the impact of hiring good people for their organization. They are uncomfortable if they hire ten people and they really can't tell you why. Once you prove to them this is a better approach because they will have reasons why they are hiring, it becomes a pretty easy sell.

What advice would you give to others who are trying to move their organization to more effective interviewing?

I think first of all you have to start with what your goal is. For us, our goal was to create the partners of the future. I think many organizations have trouble because they don't really know what they are looking for. You need to make sure you know what you want to develop in people. If you don't know what you are trying to create, it is going to be very hard for you to find it.

I would also bring in more one-on-one training earlier. I thought my first round of training would have more impact than it did. In a sense I think I underestimated how difficult it is to change the way a person conducts an interview. Three years later we found that some people didn't understand some of the basics. I think that this is a key, making sure that they know what they need to do and why they need to do it.

I have been at this for about five years. I have been trying to create this change in our interviewing approach over this period of time. I have tracked my personal recruits against the recruits of the team and I can prove that my set of recruits has produced better candidates for partner. I think that this is solely because I have had the opportunity to really understand and learn the process during the last five years where others may have been using other approaches. But I'm also seeing others getting better and that is why I continue to push to help them understand and use the process.

Susan J. Adams, Chief of Recruitment, International Monetary Fund

What were some of the key changes you made in moving your organization to a Strategic Interviewing Approach?

We have been sending our professional recruiters to the University of Michigan Strategic Interviewing Course for the past ten years. One key change has been to get more line staff involved in proper interviewing techniques to accommodate our recent push to grow the organization. At the same time, we are working to avoid "quality deterioration" in candidate selection. Retention has become a more critical factor for the organization, and this reverts back to doing the interviewing and selection better up front.

I hope our interviewing will always be evolutionary and improving, and that we did not have a "big bang" change once and for all. The only aspect I would like to have done differently in the past ten years was to have brought the University of Michigan instructors in-house to lead larger seminars tailored to all the IMF line managers, rather than simply sending our professional recruiters off-site for this important training. We are still working on this idea.

What advice would you give to others who are trying to move their organization to more effective interviewing?

The only way to get the line managers to understand the crucial role of improved interviewing is to show by example how the company can save money by better recruiting decisions. Retention figures and tracing of "bad" behaviors found in the first interviews that resulted in later performance issues are some of the techniques that might convince managers that interviewing has to be improved. Our increased rate of voluntary separations during the past five years was a wake-up call to management that we needed to do better at the first stages—the panel interview.

Coming from the line myself, I have always been skeptical of HR techniques, "flavor of the month" approaches to interviewing, and pseudoscientific methods preached by trainers in this area. But now I have to eat my words with respect to the Strategic Interviewing Approach, because it really works in our organization, and the results are so much better than what we had before!

Susan Mason, Vice President of Human Resources,
Old Kent Financial Services

What were some of the key changes you made in moving your organization to a Strategic Interviewing Approach?

We have made a number of changes to integrate Strategic Interviewing into our organization. First, our hiring managers are trained on behavior-based interviewing techniques.

Our recruiters spend more time with the job description and hiring manager to understand core competencies so they can develop effective interviewer guides. Also, recruiters are better able to identify and prioritize the candidates we decide to interview. Time spent on the front end of the hiring process has increased, but the decision process has become more efficient and effective.

What advice would you give to others who are trying to move their organization to more effective interviewing?

The advice I can give is to educate your interviewers on the importance of selecting the best candidates and how this process can help identify good talent. Help them understand that hiring good employees can reduce turnover for your company.

Applications

1. What would be the costs and benefits of implementing a Strategic Interviewing Approach in your organization?
2. What strategies can you use to build support for this approach among hiring managers?
3. Where would be the best place for you to begin using techniques from this approach to improve your interviewing process?
4. Look over the list of actions in Exhibit 7.1. What actions are likely to lead to early signs of success in implementing the Strategic Interviewing Approach in your organization?

Appendix A

Comments on Assessment 4.1

1. Tell me about a time when you were a member of a team and what your role was on the team.

   Rating: Ineffective

   Rationale: This looks like a behavioral question, but it is not closely connected to the job. The candidate may have several team examples to choose from. The question doesn't provide the candidate with any clues as to which example to present.

2. If I asked your most recent supervisor to describe you, what would he or she say?

   Rating: Ineffective

   Rationale: This question assumes that the candidate will provide a truthful answer and that there is a clear right-and-wrong set of answers. But suppose the candidate says that the supervisor would say, "We didn't get along." Is that because the candidate is hard to get along with or the supervisor?

3. Why are you the best candidate for the job?

   Rating: Ineffective

Rationale: Is this a question that the candidate should be capable of answering? Isn't it the interviewer's job to make this determination? This question measures the ability to interview rather than the ability to do the job.

4. Give me an example of a situation when you set priorities on the job. Tell me why you set them as you did.

    Rating: Ineffective

    Rationale: This is a behavioral question and it is closely connected to the job, but it is leading. It gives the answer away. A candidate knows from the question to determine priorities.

5. Have you ever had more work than could be finished by the deadline? What did you do?

    Rating: Effective

    Rationale: This is the more effective version of Question 4. It is closely connected to the job, puts the candidate in the situation, and asks about specific action.

6. Tell me about a situation in which you disagreed with your boss on handling an important issue. What did you do? Why?

    Rating: Effective

    Rationale: This is a fine question—as long as you can specify the right and wrong answers, this is the type of situation that the candidate will face on the job, and it addresses a key to success on the job.

7. Describe the most difficult problem you have faced on your previous job.

    Rating: Ineffective

    Rationale: This question is not connected to the job for which you are hiring. The most difficult problem on the previous job may have nothing to do with the types of problems in the new job. If a key to success in the new job is the candidate's ability to handle certain types of problems, either give the candidate a sample of the problem to solve or ask where the candidate has solved the specific type of problem.

8. What is your greatest accomplishment?

   Rating: Ineffective

   Rationale: Why focus on the greatest accomplishment? How can you judge if one accomplishment is better than another? Additionally, this question is not connected to the job for which the candidate is applying. What if someone said, "My greatest accomplishment is beating cancer"? This type of question might reveal some personal information that you really don't want to hear.

9. Describe a situation in which you applied your education or some knowledge learned from a different job to improve a new situation. What did you do and how did it improve the situation?

   Rating: Effective

   Rationale: This is a fine question as long as you can specify the right and wrong answers, this is the type of situation that the candidate will face on the job, and it addresses a key to success on the job.

10. Why did you select the college you attended?

    Rating: Ineffective

    Rationale: Although this question is focused on behavior, there is no tight connection between it and desired job behaviors. If the purpose of this question is to measure the ability to make job-related decisions, develop a question to measure performance on those types of decisions.

Appendix B

Sample Job Barriers, Requirements, Questions, and Answers for a Sales Position

Job Barrier—the key job situations an employee has to overcome in order to be an effective performer:

At a marketing meeting, a customer offers to close a deal if the salesperson will provide certain financial benefits.

Competency Requirements—how you would like your employees to behave in these job barrier situations:

- Quick Financial Analysis: Salesperson quickly analyzes customer's proposal and determines if it will allow an appropriate profit margin for long-term success. If so, accepts the deal. If not, proposes creative solutions that meet the customer's needs while maintaining the desired profit margin and opportunity for long-term success.

- Negotiation: Salesperson uses knowledge of the customer's needs and the capability of the salesperson's organization to identify persuasive appeals that will motivate the customer to accept the salesperson's recommendations. Comes into customer's meetings with a strategy based on such knowledge and has a variety of fallback positions. Gathers insightful market intelligence data that leads to the development of unique opportunities. Uses a negotiation strategy that shows flexibility and aims to produce win-win outcomes.

Interview Questions to Measure the Competency Requirements:

1. Have you ever been in a situation in which you proposed a deal to a customer and the customer promised you the business if you agreed to make certain changes that involved spending or providing certain financial benefits to the customer? Describe your initial proposal and the change the customer requested. What did you do and why? If you haven't been in this type of situation, describe a similar situation you have been in and how you acted. If you have not been in a similar situation, describe what you would do in this situation and why.

2. Describe a situation in which a customer promised you a deal if you gave the customer certain incentives or spent money in a certain way and you decided not to accept the recommendation. Describe the situation, what they recommended, and how you determined that the deal was not acceptable. Describe the outcome of the situation.

3. Describe a situation in which your financial analysis skills benefited your organization. I'd particularly like to hear about a situation in which you were able to think on your feet and quickly recognize the financial consequences of a proposed deal.

4. Have you ever been in a situation in which your knowledge of the customer's needs and your knowledge of the capabilities of your organization led to a unique and highly beneficial deal for your organization? Describe what you knew about the client and your own organization that led to the deal. What was the outcome?

5. Describe a situation in which you came in with a proposal to a customer that you were very high on, but that was rejected. Describe what you did in the situation and why.

6. Can you give me an example in which your market intelligence led to a unique and highly beneficial deal for your organization? Describe the market intelligence, how you obtained it, and how it benefited the deal.

Sample Answers:

Question 1

Effective: Identified the financial consequences and recognized when the customer's proposal would not meet the desired profit margin.

Ineffective: Accepted the deal without considering the financial implications of the changes or incorrectly analyzed the impact.

Question 2

Effective: Proposed financially sound creative solutions to meet the desired margin and also addressed the customer's needs.

Ineffective: Walked away from the deal without proposing creative solutions or was unable to propose alternatives that met the customer's and the organization's needs.

Question 3

Effective: Described a situation where financial skills produced a positive benefit for the organization. The situation required analyzing options and recognizing the financial consequences of the deal.

Ineffective: Provided no evidence of using financial analysis skills to produce a positive benefit to the organization.

Discussed benefits that are not clear or significant. The situation only had one option or financial consequences were not addressed.

Question 4

Effective: Used understanding of the customer's needs and the capabilities of the organization to identify unique win-win opportunities.

Ineffective: Did not come to meetings with a strategy, or came with a strategy not based on the customer's needs.

Question 5

Effective: Came to customer meetings with a strategy based upon the customer's needs and anticipated and created fallback positions that were consistent with the customer's goals.

Ineffective: Did not appear to have fallback positions or had positions that were based on the needs of the seller's organization.

Question 6

Effective: Gathered market intelligence that led to unique opportunities.

Ineffective: Showed no evidence of using market intelligence to develop unique opportunities.

Notes

Chapter One

1. P. Krugman, "Labor Pains," *New York Times Magazine* (May 23, 1999): 24.
2. C. Toris and B. M. DePaulo, "Effects of Actual Deception and Suspiciousness of Deception on Interpersonal Perceptions," *Journal of Personality and Social Psychology* 47 (1985): 1063–1073.
3. S. V. Paunon and D. N. Jackson, "Accuracy of Interviewers and Students in Identifying the Personality Characteristics of Personnel Managers and Computer Programmers," *Journal of Vocational Behavior* 31 (1987): 26–36.
4. J. F. Binning, J. M. LeBreton, and A. J. Adorno, "Assessing Personality." In *The Employment Interview Handbook,* edited by R. W. Eder and M. M. Harris. (Thousand Oaks, Calif.: Sage, 1999.)
5. R. L. Dipboye and S. L. Jackson, "Interviewer Experience and Experience Effects." In *The Employment Interview Handbook,* edited by R. W. Eder and M. M. Harris. (Thousand Oaks, Calif.: Sage, 1999.)
6. T. W. Dougherty, D. B. Turban, and J. C. Callender, "Confirming First Impressions in the Employment Interview: A Field Study of Interviewer Behavior," *Journal of Applied Psychology* 79 (1994): 659–665.

7. P. M. Rowe, "Unfavorable Information and Interviewer Decisions." In *The Employment Interview: Theory, Research and Practice,* edited by R. W. Eder and G. R. Ferris. (Thousand Oaks, Calif.: Sage, 1989.)
8. T. W. Dougherty and D. B. Turban, "Behavioral Confirmation of Interviewer Expectations." In *The Employment Interview Handbook,* edited by R. W. Eder and M. M. Harris. (Thousand Oaks, Calif.: Sage, 1999.)
9. M. M. Harris, "Reconsidering the Employment Interview: A Review of Recent Literature and Suggestions for Future Research," *Personnel Psychology* 42 (1989): 691–726.
10. R. Guion, *Assessment Measurement and Prediction for Personnel Decisions.* (Mahwah, N.J.: Erlbaum, 1998.) (Quote on pp. 609–610.)
11. M. M. Harris and R. W. Eder, "The State of Employment Interview Practice." In *The Employment Interview Handbook,* edited by R. W. Eder and M. M. Harris. (Thousand Oaks, Calif.: Sage, 1999.)
12. F. L. Schmidt and J. E. Hunter, "The Validity and Utility of Selection Measures in Personnel Psychology: Practical and Theoretical Implications of Eighty-Five Years of Research Findings," *Psychological Bulletin* 124 (1998): 262–274.

Chapter Two

1. C. K. Stevens, "Antecedents of Interview Interactions, Interviewers' Ratings, and Applicants' Reactions," *Personnel Psychology* 51 (1998): 55–85.
2. J. P. Wanous, *Organizational Entry,* 2nd ed. (Reading, Mass.: Addison-Wesley, 1992.)
3. M. Richtel, "Online Revolution's Latest Twist: Computers Screening Job Seekers," *New York Times* (February 6, 2000): 1, 19.
4. A. E. Barber, *Recruiting Employees: Individual and Organizational Perspectives.* (Thousand Oaks, Calif.: Sage, 1998.)
5. G. N. Powell and L. R. Goulet, "Recruiters and Applicant Reactions to Campus Interviews and Employment Decisions," *Academy of Management Journal* 39 (1996): 1619–1640.

6. D. B. Turban and T. W. Dougherty, "Influence of Campus Recruiting on Applicant Attraction to Firms," *Academy of Management Journal* 35 (1992): 739–765.
7. D. B. Turban, J. E. Campion, and A. R. Eyring, "Factors Related to Job Acceptance Decisions of College Recruits," *Journal of Vocational Behavior* 47 (1995): 193–213.
8. A. E. Barber, J. R. Hollenbeck, S. L. Tower, and J. M. Phillips, "The Effect of Interview Focus on Recruitment Effectiveness," *Journal of Applied Psychology* 78 (1994): 845–856.
9. D. M. Cable and T. A. Judge, "Interviewer's Perceptions of Person-Organization Fit and Organizational Selection Decisions," *Journal of Applied Psychology* 82 (1997): 546–561. See also B. Schneider, D. B. Smith, S. Taylor, and J. Fleenor, "Personality and Organizations: A Test of the Homogeneity of Personality Hypothesis," *Journal of Applied Psychology* 83 (1998): 462–470, and B. Schneider, H. W. Goldstein, and D. B. Smith, "The ASA Framework: An Update," *Personnel Psychology* 48 (1995): 747–773.
10. J. P. Wanous and A. Colella, "Organizational Entry Research: Current Status and Future Directions." In *Research in Personnel and Human Resource Management* 7, edited by K. Rowland and G. Ferris. (Greenwich, Conn.: JAI Press, 1989.)
11. S. L. Rynes, R. D. Bretz Jr., and B. Gerhart, "The Importance of Recruitment in Job Choice: A Different Way of Looking." *Personnel Psychology* 44 (1991): 487–521.

Chapter Three

1. J. C. Flanagan, "The Critical Incident Technique," *Psychological Bulletin* 51 (1954): 327–358.
2. G. P. Latham, L. M. Saari, E. D. Pursell, and M. A. Campion, "The Situational Interview," *Journal of Applied Psychology* 65 (1980): 422–427. See also T. Janz, "Initial Comparisons of Patterned Behavior Description Interviews Versus Unstructured Interviews," *Journal of Applied Psychology* 67 (1982): 577–580; and K. E. May, "Work in the Twenty-First Century: Implications for Selection," *Industrial-Organizational Psychologist* 33 (1996): 80–83.

3. H. S. Field and R. D. Gatewood, "Development of a Selection Inter-view: A Job Content Method." In *The Employment Interview: Theory, Research and Practice,* edited by R. W. Eder and G. R. Ferris. (Thousand Oaks, Calif.: Sage, 1989.) See also A. H. Church, "From Both Sides Now, the Changing of the Job," *Industrial-Organizational Psychologist* 33 (1996): 52–61.

Chapter Four

1. R. W. Eder, "Contextual Effects." In *The Employment Interview Handbook,* edited by R. W. Eder and M. M. Harris. (Thousand Oaks, Calif.: Sage, 1999.)
2. C. K. Stevens and A. L. Krisatof, "Making the Right Impression: A Field Study of Applicant Impression Management During Job Interviews," *Journal of Applied Psychology* 80 (1995): 587–606.
3. W. L. Tullar, "Relational Control in the Employment Interview," *Journal of Applied Psychology* 74 (1989): 971–977.
4. P. Wernimont and J. Campbell, "Signs, Samples, and Criteria," *Journal of Applied Psychology* 52 (1968): 372–376.
5. M. A. Campion, D. K. Palmer, and J. E. Campion, "A Review of the Structure in the Selection Interview," *Personnel Psychology* 50 (1997): 655–702.
6. M. M. Harris and R. W. Eder, "The State of Employment Interview Practice." In *The Employment Interview Handbook,* edited by R. W. Eder and M. M. Harris. (Thousand Oaks, Calif.: Sage, 1999.)
7. R. C. Liden, C. L. Martin, and C. K. Parsons, "Interviewer and Applicant Behaviors in Employment Interviews," *Academy of Management Journal* 36 (1993): 372–386.
8. F. L. Schmidt and J. E. Hunter, "The Validity and Utility of Selection Methods in Personnel Psychology," *Psychological Bulletin* 124 (1998): 262–274.
9. J. Asher and J. Sciarrino, "Realistic Work Sample Tests: A Review," *Personnel Psychology* 27 (1974): 519–533.
10. M. A. Campion, J. E. Campion, and P. J. Hudson, "Structured Interviewing: A Note on Incremental Validity and Alternative Question Types," *Journal of Applied Psychology* 79 (1994): 998–1102.

11. L. G. Williamson, J. E. Campion, S. B. Malos, M. V. Roehling, and M. A. Campion, "Employment Interview on Trial: Linking Interview Structure with Litigation Outcomes," *Journal of Applied Psychology* 82 (1997): 900–912.

Chapter Five

1. D. C. Gilmore, C. K. Stevens, G. Harrell-Cook, and G. R. Ferris, "Impression Management Tactics." In *The Employment Interview Handbook,* edited by R. W. Eder and M. M. Harris. (Thousand Oaks, Calif.: Sage, 1999.)
2. M. A. Campion, E. D. Pursell, and B. K. Brown, "Structured Interviewing: Raising the Psychometric Properties of the Employment Interview," *Personnel Psychology* 41 (1988): 25-42.
3. M. A. Campion, D. K. Palmer, and J. E. Campion, "A Review of Structure in the Selection Interview," *Personnel Psychology* 50 (1997): 655–702.
4. *Roberts* v. *Houston,* 819 F. Supp. 1019 (1993).
5. S. W. Gilliland, "Fairness From the Applicant's Perspective: Reactions to Employment Selection Procedures," *International Journal of Selection and Assessment* 3 (1995): 11–19.
6. J. Burnett, C. Fan, S. Motowidlo, and T. Degroot, "Interview Notes and Validity," *Personnel Psychology* 51 (1998): 375–396.
7. S. M. Ralston, "Applicant Communication Satisfaction, Intent to Accept Second Interview Offers, and Recruiter Communicator Style," *Journal of Applied Communication Research* 21 (1993): 53–65.
8. C. D. Mortensen, *Miscommunication.* (Thousand Oaks, Calif.: Sage, 1997.)
9. R. C. Liden, C. L. Martin, and C. K. Parsons, "Interviewer and Applicant Behaviors in Employment Interviews," *Academy of Management Journal* 36 (1993): 372–386.
10. A. Huffcutt and D. J. Woehr, "Further Analysis of Employment Interview Validity: A Quantitative Evaluation of Interviewer-Related Structuring Methods," *Journal of Organizational Behavior* 20 (1999): 549–560.

Chapter Six

1. F. L. Schmidt and M. Rader, "Exploring the Boundary Conditions for Interview Validity: Meta-Analytic Validity Findings for a New Interview Type," *Personnel Psychology* 52 (1999): 445–465.
2. A. Dalessio and A. S. Imada, "Relationship Between Interview Selection Decisions and Perceptions of Applicant Similarity to an Ideal Employee and Self: A Field Study," *Human Relations* 37 (1984): 67–80.
3. T. W. Dougherty, D. B. Turban, and J. C. Callender, "Confirming First Impressions in the Employment Interview: A Field Study," *Journal of Applied Psychology* 79 (1994): 659–665.
4. E. F. Douglas, *Straight Talk.* (Palo Alto, Calif.: Davies-Black, 1998.)
5. M. V. Roehling, J. E. Campion, and R. A. Arvey, "Unfair Discrimination Issues." In *The Employment Interview Handbook,* edited by R. W. Eder and M. M. Harris. (Thousand Oaks, Calif.: Sage, 1999.)
6. R. W. Eder and M. R. Buckley, "The Employment Interview: An Interactionist Perspective." In *Research in Personnel and Human Resource Management,* 6, edited by G. R. Ferris and K. M. Rowland. (Greenwich, Conn.: JAI, 1988.)
7. J. C. Conway, R. A. Jako, and D. Goodman, "A Meta-Analysis of Interrater and Internal Consistency Reliability of Selection Interviews," *Journal of Applied Psychology* 80 (1995): 565–579. See also A. I. Huffcutt and D. J. Woehr, "Further Analysis of Employment Interview Validity: A Quantitative Evaluation of Interviewer-Related Structuring Methods," *Journal of Organizational Behavior* 20 (1999): 549–560.
8. W. L. Tullar and P. R. Kaiser, "Using New Technology: The Group Support System." In *The Employment Interview Handbook,* edited by R. W. Eder and M. M. Harris. (Thousand Oaks, Calif.: Sage, 1999.)

The Authors

Richaurd Camp has taught strategic interviewing at the Executive Education Center of the University of Michigan Business School since 1986. He has consulted for a variety of organizations including Egon-Zehnder International, Lockheed-Martin, Fisher Scientific, Wal-Mart, Cargill, Ford, Steelcase, General Motors, and Johnson Controls.

Camp received his doctorate in industrial and organizational psychology from Wayne State University. He is a professor of management at Eastern Michigan University, where he teaches courses in staffing and training. He serves on the editorial board of the *Journal of Business and Psychology,* and is the coauthor of a book on training. He has also published in a variety of professional and practitioner journals.

Mary E. Vielhaber teaches in several programs at the Executive Education Center of the University of Michigan including Management II, Strategic Interviewing, and the Pfizer Leadership Development Program. An active consultant, she has assisted numerous organizations including Motorola, Goodyear, Detroit Edison, BASF, Pfizer, and Ford.

Vielhaber is a professor of management at Eastern Michigan University and the co-director of the Graduate Program in Human Resources and Organizational Development. She received both her M.A. and Ph.D. degrees in communication from the University of Michigan and has published articles in a variety of professional and practitioner journals.

Jack L. Simonetti is an adjunct professor of executive education at the University of Michigan, where he has taught for the past twenty years. He has been involved in hiring employees for many organizations including B.F. Goodrich, Clarklift, and the University of Toledo.

Simonetti received his doctorate from Kent State University. He has served as a professor and department chairman of management at the University of Toledo and an assistant industrial relations manager for the B.F. Goodrich Company.

In addition to numerous publications in professional and practitioner journals, he has also authored several textbooks that are used both nationally and internationally.

Index